THE THREE BRONTËS

BY

MAY SINCLAIR

First published in 1912

This edition published by Read Books Ltd.
Copyright © 2018 Read Books Ltd.
This book is copyright and may not be
reproduced or copied in any way without
the express permission of the publisher in writing

British Library Cataloguing-in-Publication Data
A catalogue record for this book is available
from the British Library

CONTENTS

PREFATORY NOTE................................5
INTRODUCTION..................................7
THE THREE BRONTËS 11
APPENDIX I 211
APPENDIX II..................................218

PREFATORY NOTE

My thanks are due, first and chiefly, to Mr. Clement K. Shorter who placed all his copyright material at my disposal; and to Mr. G.M. Williamson and Mr. Robert H. Dodd, of New York, for allowing me to draw so largely from the Poems of Emily Brontë, published by Messrs. Dodd, Mead, and Co. in 1902; also to Messrs. Hodder and Stoughton, the publishers of the Complete Poems of Emily Brontë, edited by Mr. Shorter; and to Mr. Alfred Sutro for permission to use his translation of *Wisdom and Destiny*. Lastly, and somewhat late, to Mr. Arthur Symons for his translation from St. John of the Cross. If I have borrowed from him more than I had any right to without his leave, I hope he will forgive me.

MAY SINCLAIR.

INTRODUCTION

When six months ago Mr. Thomas Seccombe suggested that I should write a short essay on "The Three Brontës" I agreed with some misgiving.

Yet that deed was innocent compared with what I have done now; and, in any case, the series afforded the offender a certain shelter and protection. But to come out like this, into the open, with *another* Brontë book, seems not only a dangerous, but a futile and a fatuous adventure. All I can say is that I did not mean to do it. I certainly never meant to write so long a book.

It grew, insidiously, out of the little one. Things happened. New criticisms opened up old questions. When I came to look carefully into Mr. Clement Shorter's collection of the *Complete Poems of Emily Brontë*, I found a mass of material (its existence I, at any rate, had not suspected) that could not be dealt with in the limits of the original essay.

The book is, and can only be, the slightest of all slight appreciations. None the less it has been hard and terrible for me to write it. Not only had I said nearly all that I had to say already, but I was depressed at the very start by that conviction of the absurdity of trying to say anything at all, after all that has been said, about Anne, or Emily, or Charlotte Brontë.

Anne's case, perhaps, was not so difficult. For obvious reasons, Anne Brontë will always be comparatively virgin soil. But it was impossible to write of Charlotte after Mrs. Gaskell; impossible to say more of Emily than Madame Duclaux has said; impossible to add one single little fact to the vast material, so patiently amassed, so admirably arranged by Mr. Clement Shorter. And when it came to appreciation there were Mr. Theodore Watts-Dunton, Sir William Robertson Nicoll, Mr. Birrell, and Mrs. Humphry Ward, lying along the ground. When it came to eulogy, after Mr. Swinburne's *Note on Charlotte Brontë*, neither Charlotte nor Emily have any need of praise.

And on Emily Brontë, M. Maeterlinck has spoken the one essential, the one perfect and final and sufficient word. I have "lifted" it unblushingly; for no other word comes near to rendering the unique, the haunting, the indestructible impression that she makes.

So, because all the best things about the Brontës have been said already, I have had to fall back on the humble day-labour of clearing away some of the rubbish that has gathered round them.

Round Charlotte it has gathered to such an extent that it is difficult to see her plainly through the mass of it. Much has been cleared away; much remains. Mrs. Oliphant's dreadful theories are still on record. The excellence of Madame Duclaux's monograph perpetuates her one serious error. Mr. Swinburne's *Note* immortalizes his. M. Héger was dug up again the other day.

It may be said that I have been calling up ghosts for the mere fun of laying them; and there might be something in it, but that really these ghosts still walk. At any rate many people believe in them, even at this time of day. M. Dimnet believes firmly that poor Mrs. Robinson was in love with Branwell Brontë. Some of us still think that Charlotte was in love with M. Héger. They cannot give him up any more than M. Dimnet can give up Mrs. Robinson.

Such things would be utterly unimportant but that they tend to obscure the essential quality and greatness of Charlotte Brontë's genius. Because of them she has passed for a woman of one experience and of one book. There is still room for a clean sweep of the rubbish that has been shot here.

In all this, controversy was unavoidable, much as I dislike its ungracious and ungraceful air. If I have been inclined to undervalue certain things—"the sojourn in Brussels", for instance—which others have considered of the first importance, it is because I believe that it is always the inner life that counts, and that with the Brontës it supremely counted.

If I have passed over the London period too lightly, it is because I judge it extraneous and external. If I have tried, cruelly, to take from Charlotte the little beige gown that she wore at Mr. Thackeray's dinner-party, it is because her home-made garments seem to suit her better. She is more herself in skirts that have brushed the moors and kept some of the soil of Haworth in their hem.

I may seem to have exaggerated her homesickness for Haworth. It may be said that Haworth was by no means Charlotte's home as it was Emily's. I am aware that there were moments—hours—when she longed to get away from it. I have not forgotten how Mary Taylor found her in such an hour, not long after her return from Brussels, when her very flesh shrank from the thought of her youth gone and "nothing done"; nothing before her but long, empty years in Haworth. The fact remains that she was never happy away from it, and that in Haworth her genius most certainly found itself at home. And this particular tone of misery and unrest disappeared from the moment when her genius declared itself, so that I am inclined to see in it a little personal dissatisfaction, if you will, but chiefly the unspeakable restlessness and misery of power unrecognized and suppressed. "Nothing done!" That was her reiterated cry.

Again, if I have overlooked the complexities of Charlotte's character, it is that the great lines that underlie it may be seen. In my heart I agree with M. Dimnet that the Brontës were not simple. All the same, I think that his admirable portrait of Charlotte is spoiled by his attitude of pity for "*la pauvre fille*", as he persists in calling her. I think he dwells a shade too much on her small asperities and acidities, and on that "*ton de critique mesquine*", which he puts down to her provincialism. No doubt there were moments of suffering and of irritation, as well as moments of uncontrollable merriment, when Charlotte lacked urbanity, but M. Dimnet has almost too keen an eye for them.

In making war on theories I cannot hope to escape a countercharge of theorizing. Exception may be taken to my own suggestion as to the effect of *Wuthering Heights* on Charlotte Brontë's genius. If anybody likes to fling it on the rubbish heap they may. I may have theorized a little too much in laying stress on the supernatural element in *Wuthering Heights*. It is because M. Dimnet has insisted too much on its brutality. I may have exaggerated Emily Brontë's "mysticism". It is because her "paganism" has been too much in evidence. It may be said that I have no more authority for my belief that Emily Brontë was in love with the Absolute than other people have for theirs, that Charlotte was in love with M. Héger.

Finally, much that I have said about Emily Brontë's hitherto unpublished poems is pure theory. But it is theory, I think, that careful examination of the poems will make good. I may have here and there given as a "Gondal" poem what is not a "Gondal" poem at all. Still, I believe, it will be admitted that it is in the cycle of these poems, and not elsewhere, that we should look for the first germs of *Wuthering Heights*. The evidence only demonstrates in detail—what has never been seriously contested—that the genius of Emily Brontë found its sources in itself.

10th October, 1911.

THE THREE BRONTËS

It is impossible to write of the three Brontës and forget the place they lived in, the black-grey, naked village, bristling like a rampart on the clean edge of the moor; the street, dark and steep as a gully, climbing the hill to the Parsonage at the top; the small oblong house, naked and grey, hemmed in on two sides by the graveyard, its five windows flush with the wall, staring at the graveyard where the tombstones, grey and naked, are set so close that the grass hardly grows between. The church itself is a burying ground; its walls are tombstones, and its floor roofs the forgotten and the unforgotten dead.

A low wall and a few feet of barren garden divide the Parsonage from the graveyard, a few feet between the door of the house and the door in the wall where its dead were carried through. But a path leads beyond the graveyard to "a little and a lone green lane", Emily Brontë's lane that leads to the open moors.

It is the genius of the Brontës that made their place immortal; but it is the soul of the place that made their genius what it is. You cannot exaggerate its importance. They drank and were saturated with Haworth. When they left it they hungered and thirsted for it; they sickened till the hour of their return. They gave themselves to it with passion, and their works ring with the shock and interchange of two immortalities. Haworth is saturated with them. Their souls are henceforth no more to be disentangled from its soul than their bodies from its earth. All their poetry, their passion and their joy is there, in this place of their tragedy, visible, palpable, narrow as the grave and boundless.

In the year eighteen-twenty the Reverend Patrick Brontë and

his wife Maria brought their six children, Maria, Elizabeth, Charlotte, Patrick Branwell, Emily, and Anne, from Thornton, where they were born, to Haworth. Mr. Brontë was an Irishman, a village schoolmaster who won, marvellously, a scholarship that admitted him to Cambridge and the Church of England. Tales have been told of his fathers and his forefathers, peasants and peasant farmers of Ballynaskeagh in County Down. They seem to have been notorious for their energy, eccentricity, imagination, and a certain tendency to turbulence and excess. Tales have been told of Mr. Brontë himself, of his temper, his egotism, his selfishness, his fits of morose or savage temper. The Brontës' biographers, from Mrs. Gaskell and Madame Duclaux[A] to Mr. Birrell, have all been hard on this poor and unhappy and innocent old man. It is not easy to see him very clearly through the multitude of tales they tell: how he cut up his wife's silk gown in a fit of passion; how he fired off pistols in a series of fits of passion; how, in still gloomier and more malignant fits, he used to go for long solitary walks. And when you look into the matter you find that the silk gown was, after all, a cotton one, and that he only cut the sleeves out, and *then* walked into Keighley and brought a silk gown back with him instead; that when he was a young man at Drumballyroney he practised pistol firing, not as a safety valve for temper but as a manly sport, and that as a manly sport he kept it up. As for solitary walks, there is really no reason why a father should not take them; and if Mr. Brontë had insisted on accompanying Charlotte and Emily in their walks, his conduct would have been censured just the same, and, I think, with considerably more reason. As it happened, Mr. Brontë, rather more than most fathers, made companions of his children when they were little. This is not quite the same thing as making himself a companion for them, and the result was a terrific outburst of infant precocity; but this hardly justifies Mrs. Gaskell and Madame Duclaux. They seem to have thought that they were somehow appeasing the outraged spirits of Emily and Charlotte by blackening their father and their brother; whereas, if anything could give pain to Charlotte and Emily and innocent Anne in heaven, it would be the knowledge of what Mrs. Gaskell and Madame Duclaux have done for them.

[Footnote A: A. Mary F. Robinson.]

There was injustice in all that zeal as well as indiscretion, for Mr. Brontë had his good points as fathers go. Think what the fathers of the Victorian era could be, and what its evangelical parsons often were; and remember that Mr. Brontë was an evangelical parson, and the father of Emily and Charlotte, not of a brood of gentle, immaculate Jane Austens, and that he was confronted suddenly and without a moment's warning with Charlotte's fame. Why, the average evangelical parson would have been shocked into apoplexy at the idea of any child of his producing *Wuthering Heights* or *Jane Eyre*. Charlotte's fame would have looked to him exceedingly like infamy. We know what Charles Kingsley, the least evangelical of parsons, once thought of Charlotte. And we know what Mr. Brontë thought of her. He was profoundly proud of his daughter's genius; there is no record and no rumour of any criticism on his part, of any remonstrance or amazement. He was loyal to Charlotte to the last days of his life, when he gave her defence into Mrs. Gaskell's hands; for which confidence Mrs. Gaskell repaid him shockingly.

But he was the kind of figure that is irresistible to the caustic or humorous biographer. There was something impotently fiery in him, as if the genius of Charlotte and Emily had flicked him in irony as it passed him by. He wound himself in yards and yards and yards of white cravat, and he wrote a revolutionary poem called "Vision of Hell". It is easy to make fun of his poems, but they were no worse, or very little worse, than his son Branwell's, so that he may be pardoned if he thought himself more important than his children. Many fathers of the Victorian era did.

And he *was* important as a temporary vehicle of the wandering creative impulse. It struggled and strove in him and passed from him, choked in yards and yards of white cravat, to struggle and strive again in Branwell and in Anne. As a rule the genius of the race is hostile to the creative impulse, and the creative impulse is lucky if it can pierce through to one member of a family. In the Brontës it emerges at five different levels, rising from abortive struggle to supreme achievement—from Mr. Brontë to his son Branwell, from Branwell to Anne, from Anne to Charlotte, and from Charlotte to Emily. And Maria, who died, was an infant prodigy.

And Mr. Brontë is important because he was the tool used by their destiny to keep Charlotte and Emily in Haworth.

The tragedy we are too apt to call their destiny began with their babyhood, when the mother and six children were brought to Haworth Parsonage and the prospect of the tombstones. They had not been there eighteen months before the mother sickened and died horribly of cancer.

She had to be isolated as far as possible. The Parsonage house was not large, and it was built with an extreme and straight simplicity; two front rooms, not large, right and left of the narrow stone-flagged passage, a bedroom above each, and between, squeezed into the small spare space above the passage, a third room, no bigger than a closet and without a fireplace. This third room is important in the story of the Brontës, for, when their mother's illness declared itself, it was in this incredibly small and insufferably unwholesome den that the five little girls were packed, heaven knows how, and it was here that the seeds of tuberculosis were sown in their fragile bodies. After their mother's death the little fatal room was known as the children's study (you can see, in a dreadful vision, the six pale little faces, pressed together, looking out of the window on to the graves below). It was used again as a night-nursery, and later still as the sleeping-place shared by two, if not three, of the sisters, two of whom were tuberculous.

The mother died and was buried in a vault under the floor of the church, not far from the windows of her house. Her sister, Miss

Branwell, came up from Penzance to look after the children. You can see this small, middle-aged, early Victorian spinster, exiled for ever from the sunshine of the town she loved, dragging out her sad, fastidious life in a cold and comparatively savage country that she unspeakably disliked. She took possession of the room her sister died in (it was the most cheerful room in the house), and lived in it. Her nieces had to sit there with her for certain hours while she taught them sewing and all the early Victorian virtues. Their father made himself responsible for the rest of their education, which he conducted with considerable vigour and originality. Maria, the eldest, was the child of promise. Long before Maria was eleven he "conversed" with her on "the leading topics of the day, with as much pleasure and freedom as with any grown-up person".

For this man, so gloomy, we are told, and so morose, found pleasure in taking his tiny children out on to the moors, where he entertained them alternately with politics and tales of brutality and horror. At six years old each little Brontë had its view of the political situation; and it was not until a plague of measles and whooping-cough found out their tender youth that their father realized how very young and small and delicate they were, and how very little, after all, he understood about a nursery. In a sudden frantic distrust of the climate of Haworth, of Miss Branwell, and his own system, he made up his mind to send Maria and Elizabeth and Charlotte and Emily to school.

And there was only one school within his means, the Clergy Daughters' School, established at Cowan Bridge in an unwholesome valley. It has been immortalized in *Jane Eyre*, together with its founder and patron, the Reverend Carus Wilson. There can be no doubt that the early Victorian virtues, self-repression, humility, and patience under affliction, were admirably taught at Cowan Bridge. And if the carnal nature of the Clergy Daughters resisted the militant efforts of Mr. Carus Wilson, it was ultimately subdued by low diet and primitive drainage working together in an unwholesome valley. Mr. Carus

Wilson, indeed, was inspired by a sublime antagonism to the claims of the perishable body; but he seems to have pushed his campaign against the flesh a bit too far, and was surprised at his own success when, one after another, the extremely perishable bodies of those children were laid low by typhus.

The fever did not touch the four little Brontës. They had another destiny. Their seed of dissolution was sown in that small stifling room at Haworth, and was reaped now at Cowan Bridge. First Maria, then Elizabeth, sickened, and was sent home to die. Charlotte stayed on for a while with Emily. She ran wild, and hung about the river, watching it, and dabbling her feet and hands in the running water. Their doom waited for Charlotte and for Emily.

There is no record of Elizabeth except that, like Anne Brontë, she was "gentle". But Maria lived in Charlotte's passionate memory, and will live for ever as Helen Burns, the school-fellow of Jane Eyre. Of those five infant prodigies, she was the most prodigious. She was the first of the children to go down into the vault under Haworth Church; you see her looking back on her sad way, a small, reluctant ghost, lovely, infantile, and yet maternal. Under her name on the flat tombstone a verse stands, premonitory, prophetic, calling to her kindred: "Be ye also ready."

Charlotte was nine years old when her sisters died. Tragedy tells at nine years old. It lived all her life in her fine nerves, reinforced by shock after shock of terror and of anguish.

But for the next seven years, spent at the Parsonage without a break, tragedy was quiescent. Day after day, year after year passed, and nothing happened. And the children of the Parsonage, thrown on themselves and on each other, were exuberantly happy. They had the freedom of the moors, and of the worlds, as wild, as gorgeous, as lonely, as immeasurable, which they themselves created. They found out that they were not obliged to be the children of the Parsonage; they could be, and they were, anything they chose, from the Duke of Wellington down to citizens of Verdopolis. For a considerable number of years they were the "Islanders". "It was in 1827" (Charlotte, at thirteen, records the date with gravity—it was so important) "that our plays were established: *Young Men*, June 1826; *Our Fellows*, July 1827; *The Islanders*, December 1827. These are our three great plays that are not kept secret."

But there were secret plays, Emily's and Charlotte's; and these you gather to be the shy and solitary flights of Emily's and Charlotte's genius. They seem to have required absolutely no impulsion from without. The difficult thing for these small children was to stop writing. Their fire consumed them, and left their bodies ashen white, fragile as ashes. And yet they were not, they could not have been, the sedentary, unwholesome little creatures they might seem to be. The girls were kept hard at work with their thin arms, brushing carpets, dusting furniture, and making beds. And for play they tramped the moors with their brother; they breasted the keen and stormy weather; the sun, the moon, the stars, and the winds knew them; and it is of these fierce, radiant, elemental things that Charlotte and Emily wrote as no women before them had ever written. Conceive the vitality and energy implied in such a life; and think, if you can, of these two as puny, myopic victims of the lust of literature. It was from the impressions they took in those seven years that their immortality was made.

And then, for a year and a half, Charlotte went to school again, that school of Miss Wooler's at Roe Head, where Ellen Nussey found her, "a silent, weeping, dark little figure in the large bay-window". She was then sixteen.

Two years later she went back to Miss Wooler's school as a teacher.

In the register of the Clergy Daughters' School there are two immortal entries:

"Charlotte Brontë.... Left school, June 1st, 1825—Governess."

"Emily Brontë.... Left, June 1st, 1825. Subsequent career—Governess."

They did not question the arrangement. They were not aware

of any other destiny. They never doubted that the boy, Branwell, was the child of promise, who was to have a glorious career. In order that he should have it the sisters left Haworth again and again, forcing themselves to the exile that destroyed them, and the work they hated. It was Charlotte and Anne who showed themselves most courageous and determined in the terrible adventure; Emily, who was courage and determination incarnate, failed. Homesickness had become a disease with them, an obsession, almost a madness. They longed with an immitigable longing for their Parsonage-house, their graveyard, and their moors. Emily was consumed by it; Anne languished; Charlotte was torn between it and her passion for knowledge.

She took Emily back with her to Roe Head as a pupil, and Emily nearly died of it. She sent Emily home, and little Anne, the last victim, took Emily's place. She and Charlotte went with the school when it was removed to Dewsbury Moor. Then Emily, who had nearly died of Roe Head, shamed by Charlotte's and Anne's example, went to Halifax as a teacher in Miss Patchett's Academy for Young Ladies. She was at Halifax—Halifax of all places—for six months, and nearly died of Halifax. And after that Charlotte and Anne set out on their careers as nursery-governesses.

It was all that they considered themselves fit for. Anne went to a Mrs. Ingham at Blake Hall, where she was homesick and miserable. Charlotte went to the Sidgwicks at Stonegappe near Skipton, where "one of the pleasantest afternoons I spent—indeed, the only one at all pleasant—was when Mr. Sidgwick walked out with his children, and I had orders to follow a little way behind". You have an impression of years of suffering endured at Stonegappe. As a matter of fact, Charlotte was there hardly three months—May, June, July, eighteen-thirty-nine.

And most of the time their brother Branwell was either at Bradford or at Haworth, dreaming of greatness, and drinking at the "Black Bull". The "Black Bull" stands disastrously near to the Parsonage, at the corner of the churchyard, with its parlour windows looking on the graves. Branwell was the life and soul of every party of commercial travellers that gathered there. Conviviality took strange forms at Haworth. It had a Masonic Lodge of the Three Graces, with John Brown, the grave-digger, for Worshipful Master. Branwell was at one and the same time secretary to the Three Graces and to the Haworth Temperance Society. When he was not entertaining bagmen, he was either at Bradford painting bad portraits, or at Haworth pouring out verses, fearfully long, fatally fluent verses, and writing hysterical letters to the editor of *Blackwood's Magazine*.

One formidable letter (the third he sent) is headed in large letters: "Sir, read what I write." It begins: "And would to Heaven you would believe in me, for then you would attend to me and act upon it", and ends: "You lost an able writer in James Hogg, and God grant you may get one in Patrick Branwell Brontë." Another followed, headed: "Sir, read now at last", and ending, "Condemn not unheard". In a final letter Branwell inquires whether Mr. Blackwood thinks his magazine "so perfect that no addition to its power would be either possible or desirable", and whether it is pride that actuates him, or custom, or prejudice, and conjures him: "Be a man, sir!"

Nothing came of it. Mr. Blackwood refused to be a man.

Yet Branwell had his chance. He went to London, but nothing came of it. He went to Bradford and had a studio there, but nothing came of it. He lived for a brief period in a small provincial Bohemia. It was his best and happiest period, but nothing came of it beyond the letters and the reams of verse he sent to Leyland the sculptor. There was something brilliant and fantastic about the boy that fascinated Leyland. But a studio costs money, and Branwell had to give his up and go back to Haworth and the society of John Brown the stone-mason and grave-digger. That John Brown was a decent fellow you gather from the fact that on a journey to Liverpool he had charge of Branwell, when Branwell was at his worst. They had affectionate names for each other. Branwell is the Philosopher, John Brown is the Old Knave of Trumps. The whole trouble with Branwell was that he could not resist the temptation of impressing the grave-digger. He himself was impressed by the ironic union in the Worshipful Master of conviviality and a sinister occupation.

A letter of Branwell's (preserved by the grave-digger in a quaint devotion to his friend's memory) has achieved an immortality denied to his "Effusions". Nothing having come of the "Effusions", Branwell, to his infinite credit, followed his sisters' example, and became tutor with a Mr. Postlethwaite. The irony of his situation pleased him, and he wrote to the Old Knave of Trumps thus: "I took a half-year's farewell of old friend whisky at Kendal on the night after I left. There was a party of gentlemen at the Royal Hotel, and I joined them. We ordered in supper and whisky-toddy as hot as hell! They thought I was a physician, and put me in the chair. I gave several toasts that were washed down at the same time till the room spun round and the candles danced in our eyes.... I found myself in bed next morning with a bottle of porter, a glass, and a corkscrew beside me. Since then I have not tasted anything stronger than milk-and-water, nor, I hope, shall, till I return at midsummer; when we will see about it. I am getting as fat as Prince William at Springhead, and as godly as his friend Parson Winterbotham. My hand shakes no longer. I ride to the banker's at Ulverston with Mr. Postlethwaite, and sit drinking tea, and talking scandal with old ladies. As for the young ones! I have one sitting by me just now—fair-faced, blue-eyed, dark-haired, sweet eighteen—she little thinks the devil is so near her!"—and a great deal more in the same silly, post-Byronic strain.

In his postscript Branwell says: "Of course you won't show this letter", and of course John Brown showed it all round. It was far too good to be kept to himself; John Brown's brother thought it so excellent that he committed it to memory. This was hard on Branwell. The letter is too fantastic to be used against him as evidence of his extreme depravity, but it certainly lends some support to Mrs. Gaskell's statements that he had begun already, at two-and-twenty, to be an anxiety to his family. Haworth, that schooled his sisters to a high and beautiful austerity, was bad for Branwell.

He stayed with Mr. Postlethwaite for a month longer than Charlotte stayed with the Sidgwicks.

Then, for a whole year, Charlotte was at Haworth, doing housemaid's work, and writing poems, and amusing herself at the expense of her father's curates. She had begun to find out the extent to which she could amuse herself. She also had had "her chance". She had refused two offers of marriage, preferring the bondage and the exile that she knew. Nothing more exhilarating than a proposal that you have rejected. Those proposals did Charlotte good. But it was not marriage that she wanted. She found it (for a year) happiness enough to be at Haworth, to watch the long comedy of the curates as it unrolled itself before her. She saw most things that summer (her twenty-fifth) with the ironic eyes of the comic spirit, even Branwell. She wrote to Miss Nussey: "A distant relation of mine, one Patrick Boanerges, has set off to seek his fortune in the wild, wandering, knight-errant-like capacity of clerk on the Leeds and Manchester Railroad." And she goes on to chaff Miss Nussey about Celia Amelia, the curate. "I know Mrs. Ellen is burning with eagerness to hear something about W. Weightman, whom she adores in her heart, and whose image she cannot efface from her memory."

Some of her critics, including Mrs. Oliphant (far less indulgent than the poor curates who forgave her nobly), have grudged Charlotte her amusement. There is nothing, from her fame downwards, that Mrs. Oliphant did not grudge her. Mr. Birrell sternly disapproves; even Mr. Swinburne, at the height of his panegyric, is put off. Perhaps Charlotte's humour was not her most attractive quality; but nobody seems to have seen the pathos and the bravery of it. Neither have they seen that Miss Nussey was at the bottom of its worst development, the "curate-baiting". Miss Nussey used to go and stay at Haworth for weeks at a time. Haworth was not amusing, and Miss Nussey had to be amused. All this school-girlish jesting, the perpetual and rather tiresome banter, was a playing down to Miss Nussey. It was a kind of tender "baiting" of Miss Nussey, who had tried on several occasions to do Charlotte good. And it was the natural, healthy rebound of the little Irish *gamine* that lived in Charlotte Brontë, bursting with cleverness and devilry. I, for my part, am glad to think that for one happy year she gave it full vent.

She was only twenty-four. Even as late as the mid-Victorian era to be twenty-four and unmarried was to be middle-aged. But (this cannot be too much insisted on) Charlotte Brontë was the revolutionist who changed all that. She changed it not only in her novels but in her person. Here again she has been misrepresented. There are no words severe enough for Mrs. Oliphant's horrible portrait of her as a plain-faced, lachrymose, middle-aged spinster, dying, visibly, to be married, obsessed for ever with that idea, for ever whining over the frustration of her sex. What Mrs. Oliphant, "the married woman", resented in Charlotte Brontë, over and above her fame, was Charlotte's unsanctioned knowledge of the mysteries, her intrusion into the veiled places, her unbaring of the virgin heart. That her genius was chiefly concerned in it does not seem to have occurred to Mrs. Oliphant, any more than it occurred to her to notice the impression that Charlotte Brontë made on her male contemporaries. It is doubtful if one of them thought of her as Mrs. Oliphant would have us think. They gave her the tender, deferent affection they would have given to a charming child. Even the very curates saw in her, to their amazement, the spirit of undying youth. Small as a child, and fragile, with soft hair and flaming eyes, and always the pathetic, appealing plainness of a plain child, with her child's audacity and shyness, her sudden, absurd sallies and retreats, she had a charm made the more piquant by her assumption of austerity. George Henry Lewes was gross and flippant, and he could not see it; Branwell's friend, Mr. Grundy, was Branwell's friend, and he missed it. Mrs. Oliphant ranges herself with Mr. Grundy and George Henry Lewes.

But Charlotte's fun was soon over, and she became a nursery-governess again at Mrs. White's, of Rawdon. Anne was with Mrs. Robinson, at Thorp Green.

Emily was at Haworth, alone.

That was in eighteen-forty-one. Years after their death a little black box was found, containing four tiny scraps of paper, undiscovered by Charlotte when she burnt every line left by Anne and Emily except their poems. Two of these four papers were written by Emily, and two by Anne; each sister keeping for the other a record of four years. They begin in eighteen-forty-one. Emily was then twenty-four and Anne a year and a half younger. Nothing can be more childlike, more naïve. Emily heads her diary:

> A PAPER to be opened
> when Anne is
> 25 years old,
> or my next birthday after
> if
> all be well.
> Emily Jane Brontë. July the 30th, 1841.

She says: "It is Friday evening, near nine o'clock—wild rainy weather. I am seated in the dining-room, having just concluded tidying our desk-boxes, writing this document. Papa is in the parlour—Aunt upstairs in her room.... Victoria and Adelaide are ensconced in the peat-house. Keeper is in the kitchen—Hero in his cage."

Having accounted for Victoria and Adelaide, the tame geese, Keeper, the dog, and Hero, the hawk, she notes the whereabouts of Charlotte, Branwell, and Anne. And then (with gravity):

"A scheme is at present in agitation for setting us up in a school of our own."... "This day four years I wonder whether we shall be dragging on in our present condition or established to our hearts' content."

Then Emily dreams her dream.

"I guess that on the time appointed for the opening of this paper we, *i.e.* Charlotte, Anne, and I, shall be all merrily seated in our own sitting-room in some pleasant and flourishing seminary, having just gathered in for the midsummer holiday. Our debts will be paid off and we shall have cash in hand to a considerable amount. Papa, Aunt, and Branwell, will either have been or be coming to visit us."

And Anne writes with equal innocence (it is delicious, Anne's diary): "Four years ago I was at school. Since then I have been a governess at Blake Hall, left it, come to Thorp Green, and seen the sea and York Minster."... "We have got Keeper, got a sweet little cat and lost it, and also got a hawk. Got a wild goose which has flown away, and three tame ones, one of which has been killed."

It is Emily who lets out the dreary secret of the dream—the debts which could not be paid; probably Branwell's.

But the "considerable amount of cash in hand" was to remain a dream. Nothing came of Branwell's knight-errantry. He muddled the accounts of the Leeds and Manchester Railroad and was sent home. It was not good for Branwell to be a clerk at a lonely wayside station. His disaster, which they much exaggerated, was a shock to the three sisters. They began to have misgivings, premonitions of Branwell's destiny.

And from Mrs. White's at Rawdon, Charlotte sends out cry after desolate cry. Again we have an impression of an age of exile, but really the exile did not last long, not much longer than Emily's imprisonment in the Academy for Young Ladies, nothing like so long as Anne's miserable term.

The exile really began in 'forty-two, when Charlotte and Emily left England for Brussels and Madame Héger's Pensionnat de Demoiselles in the Rue d'Isabelle. It is supposed to have been the turning-point in Charlotte's career. She was then twenty-six, Emily twenty-four.

It is absurd and it is pathetic, but Charlotte's supreme ambition at that time was to keep a school, a school of her own, like her friend Miss Wooler. There was a great innocence and humility in

Charlotte. She was easily taken in by any of those veiled, inimical spectres of the cross-roads that youth mistakes for destiny. She must have refused to look too closely at the apparition; it was enough for her that she saw in it the divine thing—liberty. Her genius was already struggling in her. She had begun to feel under her shoulders the painful piercing of her wings. Her friend, Mary Taylor, had written to her from Brussels telling her of pictures and cathedrals. Charlotte tells how it woke her up. "I hardly know what swelled in my breast as I read her letter: such a vehement impatience of restraint and steady work; such a strong wish for wings—wings such as wealth can furnish; such an urgent desire to see, to know, to learn; something internal seemed to expand bodily for a minute. I was tantalized by the consciousness of faculties unexercised." But Charlotte's "wings" were not "such as wealth can furnish". They were to droop, almost to die, in Brussels.

Emily was calmer. Whether she mistook it for her destiny or not, she seems to have acquiesced when Charlotte showed her the veiled figure at the cross-roads, to have been led blindfold by Charlotte through the "streaming and starless darkness" that took them to Brussels. The rest she endured with a stern and terrible resignation. It is known from her letters what the Pensionnat was to Charlotte. Heaven only knows what it must have been to Emily. Charlotte, with her undying passion for knowledge and the spectacle of the world, with her psychological interest in M. Héger and his wife, Charlotte hardly came out of it with her soul alive. But Emily was not interested in M. Héger nor in his wife, nor in his educational system. She thought his system was no good and told him so. What she thought of his wife is not recorded.

Then, in their first year of Brussels, their old aunt, Miss Branwell, died. That was destiny, the destiny that was so kind to Emily. It sent her and her sister back to Haworth and it kept her there. Poor Anne was fairly launched on her career; she remained in her "situation", and somebody had to look after Mr. Brontë and the house. Things were going badly and sadly at the Parsonage. Branwell was there, drinking; and Charlotte was even afraid that her father ... also sometimes ... perhaps....

She left Emily to deal with them and went back to Brussels as a pupil teacher, alone. She went in an agony of self-reproach, desiring more and more knowledge, a perfect, inalienable, indestructible possession of the German language, and wondering whether it were right to satisfy that indomitable craving. By giving utterance to this self-reproach, so passionate, so immense, so disproportioned to the crime, the innocent Charlotte laid herself open to an unjust suspicion. Innocent and unaware she went, and—it is her own word—she was "punished" for it.

Nothing that she had yet known of homesickness could compare with that last year of solitary and unmitigated exile. It is supposed, even by the charitable, that whatever M. Héger did or did not do for Charlotte, he did everything for her genius. As a matter of fact, it was at Brussels that she suffered the supreme and ultimate abandonment. She no longer felt the wild unknown thing stirring in her with wings. So little could M. Héger do for it that it refused to inhabit the same house with him. She records the result of that imprisonment a few weeks after her release: "There are times now when it appears to me as if all my ideas and feelings, except a few friendships and affections, are changed from what they used to be; something in me, which used to be enthusiasm, is tamed down and broken."

At Brussels surely enlightenment must have come to her. She must have seen, as Emily saw, that in going that way, she had mistaken and done violence to her destiny.

She went back to Haworth where it waited for her, where it had turned even the tragedy of her family to account. Everything conspired to keep her there. The school was given up. She tells why. "It is on Papa's account; he is now, as you know, getting old, and it grieves me to tell you that he is losing his sight. I have felt for some months that I ought not to be away from him; and

I feel now that it would be too selfish to leave (at least as long as Branwell and Anne are absent) to pursue selfish interests of my own. With the help of God I will try to deny myself in this matter, and to wait."

And with the help of God she waited.

There are three significant entries in Emily's sealed paper for eighteen-forty-five. "Now I don't desire a school at all, and none of us have any great longing for it." "I am quite contented for myself ... seldom or never troubled with nothing to do and merely desiring that everybody could be as comfortable as myself and as undesponding, and then we should have a very tolerable world of it." "I have plenty of work on hand, and writing...." This, embedded among details of an incomparable innocence: "We have got Flossy; got and lost Tiger; lost the hawk, Hero, which, with the geese, was given away, and is doubtless dead."

And Anne, as naïve as a little nun, writes in *her* sealed paper: "Emily is upstairs ironing. I am sitting in the dining-room in the rocking-chair before the fire with my feet on the fender. Papa is in the parlour. Tabby and Martha are, I think, in the kitchen. Keeper and Flossy are, I do not know where. Little Dick is hopping in his cage." And then, "Emily ... is writing some poetry.... I wonder what it is about?"

That is the only clue to the secret that is given. These childlike diaries are full of the "Gondal Chronicles",[A] an interminable fantasy in which for years Emily collaborated with Anne. They flourished the "Gondal Chronicles" in each other's faces, with positive bravado, trying to see which could keep it up the longer. Under it all there was a mystery; for, as Charlotte said of their old play, "Best plays were secret plays," and the sisters kept their best hidden. And then suddenly the "Gondal Chronicles" were dropped, the mystery broke down. All three of them had been writing poems; they had been writing poems for years. Some of Emily's dated from her first exile at Roe Head. Most of Anne's sad songs were sung in her house of bondage. From Charlotte, in her Brussels period, not a line.

[Footnote A: See *supra*, pp. 193 to 209.]

But at Haworth, in the years that followed her return and found her free, she wrote nearly all her maturer poems (none of them were excessively mature): she wrote *The Professor*, and close upon *The Professor*, *Jane Eyre*. In the same term that found her also, poor child, free, and at Haworth, Anne wrote *Agnes Grey* and *The Tenant of Wildfell Hall*.

And Emily wrote *Wuthering Heights*.

They had found their destiny—at Haworth.

* * * * *

Every conceivable theory has been offered to account for the novels that came so swiftly and incredibly from these three sisters. It has been said that they wrote them merely to pay their debts when they found that poems did not pay. It would be truer to say that they wrote them because it was their destiny to write them, and because their hour had come, and that they published them with the dimmest hope of a return.

Before they knew where they were, Charlotte found herself involved in what she thought was a businesslike and masculine correspondence with publishing firms.

The *Poems* by Currer, Ellis, and Acton Bell, appeared first, and nothing happened. *The Professor* travelled among publishers, and nothing happened. Then, towards the end of the fourth year there came *Jane Eyre*, and Charlotte was famous.

But not Emily. *Wuthering Heights* appeared also, and nothing happened. It was bound in the same volume with Anne's humble tale. Its lightning should have scorched and consumed *Agnes Grey*, but nothing happened. Ellis and Acton Bell remained equals in obscurity, recognized only by their association with the tremendous Currer. When it came to publishing *The Tenant of Wildfell Hall*, and association became confusion, Charlotte and Anne went up to London to prove their separate identity. Emily stayed at Haworth, superbly indifferent to the proceedings. She was unseen, undreamed of, unrealized, and in all her life she made no sign.

But, in a spirit of reckless adventure, Charlotte and Anne walked the seven miles to Keighley on a Friday evening in a thunderstorm, and took the night train up. On the Saturday morning they appeared in the office at Cornhill to the amazement of Mr. George Smith and Mr. Williams. With childlike innocence and secrecy they hid in the Chapter Coffee-house in Paternoster Row, and called themselves the Misses Brown. When entertainment was offered them, they expressed a wish to hear Dr. Croly preach. They did not hear him; they only heard *The Barber of Seville* at Covent Garden. They tried, with a delicious solemnity, to give the whole thing an air of business, but it was really a breathless, infantile escapade of three days. Three days out of four years.

* * * * *

And in those four years poor Branwell's destiny found him also. After many minor falls and penitences and relapses, he seemed at length to have settled down. He had been tutor for two and a half years with the Robinsons at Thorp Green, in the house where Anne was a governess. He was happy at first; an ominous happiness. Then Anne began to be aware of something.

Mr. Birrell has said rather unkindly that he has no use for this young man. Nobody had any use for him. Not the editors to whom he used to write so hysterically. Not the Leeds and Manchester Railroad Company. And certainly not Mrs. Robinson, the lady for whom he conceived that insane and unlawful passion which has been made to loom so large in the lives of the Brontës. After all the agony and indignation that has gathered round this episode, it is clear enough now, down to the last sordid details. The feverish, degenerate, utterly irresponsible Branwell not only declared his passion, but persuaded himself, against the evidence of his senses, that it was returned. The lady (whom he must have frightened horribly) told her husband, who instantly dismissed Branwell.

Branwell never got over it.

He was destined to die young, and, no doubt, if there had been no Mrs. Robinson, some other passion would have killed him. Still, it may be said with very little exaggeration that he died of it. He had not hitherto shown any signs of tuberculosis. It may be questioned whether without this predisposing cause he would have developed it. He had had his chance to survive. *He* had never been packed, like his sisters, first one of five, then one of three, into a closet not big enough for one. But he drank harder after the Robinson affair than he had ever drunk before, and he added opium to drink. Drink and opium gave frightful intensity to the hallucination of which, in a sense, he died.

It took him more than three years, from July, eighteen-forty-five, the date of his dismissal, to September, eighteen-forty-eight, the date of his death.

The Incumbent of Haworth has been much blamed for his son's shortcomings. He has been charged with first spoiling the boy, and then neglecting him. In reality his only error (a most unusual one in an early Victorian father) was that he believed in his son's genius. When London and the Royal Academy proved beyond him he had him taught at Bradford. He gave him a studio there. He had already given him an education that at least enabled him to obtain tutorships, if not to keep them. The Parsonage must have been a terrible place for Branwell, but it was not in the Vicar's power to make it more attractive than the Bull Inn. Branwell was not a poet like his sisters, and moors meant nothing to him. To be sure, when he went into Wales and saw Penmaenmawr, he wrote a poem about it. But the poem is not really about Penmaenmawr. It is all about Branwell; Penmaenmawr *is* Branwell, a symbol of his colossal personality and of his fate. For Branwell was a monstrous egoist. He was not interested in his sisters or in his friends, or really in Mrs.

Robinson. He was interested only in himself. What could a poor vicar do with a son like that? There was nothing solid in Branwell that you could take hold of and chastise. There was nothing you could appeal to. His affection for his family was three-fourths sentimentalism. Still, what the Vicar could do he did do. When Branwell was mad with drink and opium he never left him. There is no story more grim and at the same time more poignant and pathetic than that which Mrs. Gaskell tells of his devotion to his son in this time of the boy's ruin. Branwell slept in his father's room. He would doze all day, and rage all night, threatening his father's life. In the morning he would go to his sisters and say: "The poor old man and I have had a terrible night of it. He does his best, the poor old man, but it is all over with me." He died in his father's arms while Emily and little Anne looked on.

They say that he struggled to his feet and died standing, to prove the strength of his will; but some biographer has robbed him of this poor splendour. It was enough for his sisters—and it should be enough for anybody—that his madness left him with the onset of his illness, and that he went from them penitent and tender, purified by the mystery and miracle of death.

That was on Sunday, the twenty-fourth of September. From that day Emily sickened. She caught cold at Branwell's funeral. On September the thirtieth she was in church listening to his funeral sermon. After that, she never crossed the threshold of the Parsonage till in December her dead body was carried over it, to lie beside her brother under the church floor.

In October, a week or two after Branwell's death, Charlotte wrote: "Emily has a cold and cough at present." "Emily's cold and cough are very obstinate. I fear she has pain in her chest, and I sometimes catch a shortness in her breathing when she has moved at all quickly." In November: "I told you Emily was ill, in my last letter. She has not rallied yet. She is very ill.... I think Emily seems the nearest thing to my heart in all the world." And in December: "Emily suffers no more from pain or weakness now ... there is no Emily in time, or on earth now.... We are very calm at present. Why should we be otherwise? The anguish of seeing her suffer is over; the spectacle of the pains of death is gone by: the funeral day is past. We feel she is at peace. No need to tremble for the hard frost and the keen wind. Emily does not feel them. She died in a time of promise.... But it is God's will, and the place where she has gone is better than that which she has left."

It could have been hardly daylight on the moors the morning when Charlotte went out to find that last solitary sprig of heather which she laid on Emily's pillow for Emily to see when she awoke. Emily's eyes were so drowsed with death that she could not see it. And yet it could not have been many hours later when a fire was lit in her bedroom, and she rose and dressed herself. Madame Duclaux[A] tells how she sat before the fire, combing her long, dark hair, and how the comb dropped from her weak fingers, and fell under the grate. And how she sat there in her mortal apathy; and how, when the servant came to her, she said dreamily: "Martha, my comb's down there; I was too weak to stoop and pick it up."

[Footnote A: "Emily Brontë": *Eminent Women Series*.]

She dragged herself down to the sitting-room, and died there, about two o'clock. She must have had some horror of dying in that room of death overhead; for, at noon, when the last pains seized her, she refused to be taken back to it. Unterrified, indomitable, driven by her immortal passion for life, she fought terribly. Death took her as she tried to rise from the sofa and break from her sisters' arms that would have laid her there. Profoundly, piteously alienated, she must have felt that Anne and Charlotte were in league with death; that they fought with her and bound her down; and that in her escape from them she conquered.

Another month and Anne sickened. As Emily died of Branwell's death, so Emily's death hastened Anne's. Charlotte wrote in the middle of January: "I can scarcely say that Anne is worse, nor can I say she is better.... The days pass in a slow, dull march: the nights are the test; the sudden wakings from restless sleep, the revived knowledge that one lies in her grave, and another, not at my side, but in a separate and sick bed." And again in March: "Anne's decline is gradual and fluctuating, but its nature is not doubtful." And yet again in April: "If there were no hope beyond this world ... Emily's fate, and that which threatens Anne, would be heartbreaking. I cannot forget Emily's death-day; it becomes a more fixed, a darker, a more frequently recurring idea in my mind than ever. It was very terrible. She was torn, conscious, panting, reluctant, though resolute, out of a happy life."

Mrs. Oliphant has censured Emily Brontë for the manner of her dying. She might as well have censured Anne for drawing out the agony. For Anne was gentle to the end, utterly submissive. She gave death no trouble. She went, with a last hope, to Scarborough, and died there at the end of May. She was buried at Scarborough, where she lies alone. It is not easy to believe that she had no "preference for place", but there is no doubt that even to that choice of her last resting-place she would have submitted—gently.

"I got here a little before eight o'clock. All was clean and bright, waiting for me. Papa and the servants were well, and all received me with an affection that should have consoled. The dogs seemed in strange ecstasy. I am certain that they regarded me as the harbinger of others. The dumb creatures thought that as I was returned, those who had been so long absent were not far behind.... I felt that the house was all silent, the rooms were all empty. I remembered where the three were laid—in what narrow, dark dwellings—never more to reappear on earth.... I cannot help thinking of their last days, remembering their sufferings, and what they said and did, and how they looked in mortal affliction.... To sit in a lonely room, the clock ticking loud through a still house...." Charlotte could see nothing else before her.

It was July. She had come home after a visit to Miss Nussey.

In that month she wrote that chapter of *Shirley* which is headed "The Valley of the Shadow". The book (begun more than eighteen months before) fairly quivers with the shock that cut it in two.

It was finished somewhere in September of that year of Anne's death. Charlotte went up to London. She saw Thackeray. She learned to accept the fact of her celebrity.

Somehow the years passed, the years of Charlotte's continuous celebrity, and of those literary letters that take so disproportionate a part in her correspondence that she seems at last to have forgotten; she seems to belong to the world rather than to Haworth. And the world seems full of Charlotte; the world that had no place for Emily. And yet *Wuthering Heights* had followed *Shirley*. It had been republished with Charlotte's introduction, her vindication of Emily. It brought more fame for Charlotte, but none—yet—for Emily.

Two years later came *Villette*. Charlotte went up to London a second time and saw Thackeray again. And there were more letters, the admirable but slightly self-conscious letters of the literary woman, artificially assured. They might deceive you, only the other letters, the letters to Ellen Nussey go on; they come palpitating with the life of Charlotte Brontë's soul that had in it nothing of the literary taint. You see in them how, body and soul, Haworth claims her and holds her, and will not let her go.

Nor does she desire now to be let go. Her life at Haworth is part of Emily's life; it partakes of the immortality of the unforgotten dead. London and Thackeray, the Smiths, Mrs. Gaskell, and Miss Martineau, Sir John and Lady Kay-Shuttleworth, her celebrity and the little train of cheerful, unfamiliar circumstances, all these things sink into insignificance beside it. They are all extraneous somehow, and out of keeping. Nothing that her biographers have done (when they have done their worst) can destroy or even diminish the effect her life gives of unity, of fitness, of profound and tragic harmony. It was Mrs. Gaskell's sense of this effect that made her work a masterpiece.

And in her marriage, at Haworth, to her father's curate, Arthur Nicholls, the marriage that cut short her life and made an end of her celebrity, Charlotte Brontë followed before all things her instinct for fitness, for unity, for harmony. It was exquisitely in keeping. It did no violence to her memories, her simplicities and sanctities. It found her in the apathy of exhaustion, and it was yet one with all that was passionate in her and undying. She went to it one morning in May, all white and drooping, in her modest gown and that poor little bridal bonnet with its wreath of snowdrops, symbolic of all the timidities, the reluctances, the cold austerities of spring roused in the lap of winter, and yet she found in it the secret fire of youth. She went to it afraid; and in her third month of marriage she still gives a cry wrung from the memory of her fear. "Indeed, indeed, Nell, it is a solemn and strange and perilous thing for a woman to become a wife."

And yet for all that, after London, after fame and friendships in which her dead had no share, her marriage was not the great departure; it was the great return. It was the outcome of all that had gone before it; the fruit of painful life, which is recognition, acceptance, the final trust in destiny. There were to be no more false starts, no more veiled ghosts of the cross-roads, pointing the disastrous way.

And in its abrupt and pitiful end her life rang true; it sustained the tragic harmony. It was the fulfilment of secret prophecies, forebodings, premonitions, of her reiterated "It was not to be." You may say that in the end life cheated and betrayed her.

And inevitably; for she had loved life, not as Emily loved it, like an equal, with power over it and pride and an unearthly understanding, virgin and unafraid. There was something slightly subservient, consciously inferior, in Charlotte's attitude to life. She had loved it secretly, with a sort of shame, with a corroding passion and incredulity and despair. Such natures are not seldom victims of the power they would propitiate. It killed her in her effort to bring forth life.

When the end came she could not realize it. For the first time she was incredulous of disaster. She heard, out of her last stupor, her husband praying that God would spare her, and she whispered, "Oh, I am not going to die, am I? He will not separate us; we have been so happy."

You can see her youth rising up beside that death-bed and answering, "That is why."

And yet, could even Charlotte's youth have been so sure as to the cheating and betrayal? That happiness of hers was cut short in the moment of its perfection. She was not to suffer any disenchantment or decline; her love was not to know any cold of fear or her genius any fever of frustration. She was saved the struggle we can see before her. Arthur Nicholls was passionately fond of Charlotte. But he was hostile to Charlotte's genius and to Charlotte's fame. A plain, practical, robust man, inimical to any dream. He could be adorably kind to a sick, submissive Charlotte. Would he have been so tender to a Charlotte in revolt? She was spared the torture of the choice between Arthur Nicholls and her genius. We know how she would have chosen. It is well for her, and it is all one to literature, that she died, not "in a time of promise", but in the moment of fulfilment.

*****

No. Of these tragic Brontës the most tragic, the most pitiful, the most mercilessly abused by destiny, was Anne. An interminable, monstrous exile is the impression we get of Anne's life in the years of her girlhood. There is no actual record of them. Nobody kept Anne's letters. We never hear her sad voice raised in self-pity or revolt. It is doubtful if she ever raised it. She waited in silence and resignation, and then told her own story in *Agnes Grey*. But her figure remains dim in her own story and in the classic "Lives". We only know that she was the youngest, and that, unlike her sisters, she was pretty. She had thick brown curling hair, and violet-blue eyes, and delicate dark eyebrows, and a skin rose and white for her sisters' sallow, that must have given some ominous hint of fever. This delicate thing was broken on the wheel of life. They say of Anne perpetually that she was "gentle". In Charlotte's sketch of her she holds her pretty head high, her eyes gaze straight forward, and you wonder whether, before the breaking point, she was always as gentle as they say. But you never see her in any moment of revolt. Her simple poems, at their bitterest, express no more than a frail agony, an innocent dismay. That little raising of the head in conscious rectitude is all that breaks the long plaint of *Agnes Grey*.

There is no piety in that plaint. It is purely pagan; the cry of youth cheated of its desire. Life brought her no good gifts beyond the slender ineffectual beauty that left her undesired. Her tremulous, expectant womanhood was cheated. She never saw so much as the flying veil of joy, or even of such pale, uninspired happiness as she dreamed in *Agnes Grey*. She was cheated of her innocent dream.

And by an awful irony her religion failed her. She knew its bitterness, its terrors, its exactions. She never knew its ecstasies, its flaming mysteries, nor, even at her very last, its consolations. Her tender conscience drew an unspeakable torment from the spectacle of her brother's degradation.

For it was on Anne, who had no genius to sustain her, that poor Branwell, with the burden of his destiny, weighed most hard. It was Anne at Thorp Green who had the first terrible misgivings, the intolerable premonitions.

That wretched story is always cropping up again. The lady whom Mrs. Gaskell, with a murderous selection of adjectives, called "that mature and wicked woman", has been cleared as far as evidence and common sense could clear her. But the slander is perpetually revived. It has always proved too much for the Brontë biographers. Madame Duclaux published it again twenty years after, in spite of the evidence and in spite of Mrs. Gaskell's retractation. You would have thought that Branwell might have been allowed to rest in the grave he dug for himself so well.

But no, they will not let him rest. Branwell drank, and he ate opium; and, as if drink and opium and erotic madness were not enough, they must credit him with an open breach of the seventh commandment as well. M. Dimnet, the most able of recent critics of the Brontës, thinks and maintains against all evidence that there was more in it than Branwell's madness. He will not give up the sordid tragedy *à trois*. He thinks he knows what Anne thought of Branwell's behaviour, and what awful secret she was hinting at, and what she told her sisters when she came back to Haworth. He argues that Anne Brontë saw and heard things, and that her testimony is not to be set aside.

What did Anne Brontë see and hear? She saw her brother consumed by an illegitimate passion; a passion utterly hopeless, given the nature of the lady. The lady had been kind to Anne, to Branwell she had been angelically kind. Anne saw that his behaviour was an atrocious return for her kindness. Further than that the lady hardly counted in Anne's vision. Her interest was centred on her brother. She saw him taking first to drink and then to opium. She saw that he was going mad, and he did go mad. One of the most familiar symptoms of morphia mania is a tendency to erotic hallucinations of the precise kind that Branwell suffered from. Anne was unable to distinguish between such a hallucination and depravity. But there is not a shadow of evidence that she thought what M. Dimnet thinks, or that if she had thought it she made Charlotte and Emily think it too. Branwell's state was quite enough in itself to break their hearts. His letters to Leyland, to John Brown, the sexton, to Francis Grundy, record with frightful vividness every phase of his obsession.

It is inconceivable that such letters should have been kept, still more inconceivable that they should have been published. It is inconceivable that Mrs. Gaskell should have dragged the pitiful and shameful figure into the light. Nobody can save poor Branwell now from the dreadful immortality thrust on him by his enemies and friends with equal zeal. All that is left to us is a merciful understanding of his case. Branwell's case, once for all, was purely pathological. There was nothing great about him, not even his passion for Mrs. Robinson. Properly speaking, it was not a passion at all, it was a disease. Branwell was a degenerate, as incapable of passion as he was of poetry. His sisters, Anne and Charlotte, talked with an amazing innocence about Branwell's vices. Simple and beautiful souls, they never for a moment suspected that his worst vice was sentimentalism. In the beginning, before it wrecked him, nobody enjoyed his own emotions more than Branwell. At his worst he wallowed voluptuously in the torments of frustration. At the end, what with drink and what with opium, he was undoubtedly insane. His letters are priceless pathological documents. They reveal all the workings of his peculiar mania. He thinks everybody is plotting to keep him from Mrs. Robinson. Faced at every turn with the evidence of this lady's complete indifference, he gives it all a lunatic twist to prove the contrary. He takes the strangest people into his confidence, John Brown, the sexton, and the Robinsons' coachman. Queer flames of lucidity dart here and there through this madness: "The probability of her becoming free to give me herself and estate ever rose to drive away the prospect of her decline under her present grief." "I had reason to hope that ere very long I should be the husband of a lady whom I loved best in the world, and with whom, in more than competence, I might live at leisure to try to make myself a name in the world of posterity, without being pestered by the small but countless botherments, which, like mosquitoes, sting us in the world of work-day toil. That hope and herself are gone—she to wither into patiently pining decline—*it* to make room for drudgery." It is all sordid as well as terrible. We have no right to know these things. Mrs. Oliphant is almost justified in her protest against Charlotte as the first to betray her brother.

But did Charlotte betray Branwell? Not in her letters. She never imagined—how could she?—that those letters would be published. Not in her novels. Her novels give no portrait of Branwell and no hint that could be easily understood. It is in her prefaces to her sisters' novels that he appears, darkly. Charlotte, outraged by the infamous article in the *Quarterly*, was determined that what had been said of her should never be said of Anne and Emily. She felt that their works offered irresistible provocation to the scandalous reviewer. She thought it necessary to explain how they came by their knowledge of evil.

This vindication of her sisters is certainly an indictment of her brother to anybody who knew enough to read between the lines. Charlotte may have innocently supposed that nobody knew or ever would know enough. Unfortunately, Mrs. Gaskell knew; and when it came to vindicating Charlotte, she considered herself justified in exposing Charlotte's brother because Charlotte herself had shown her the way.

But Charlotte might have spared her pains. Branwell does not account for Heathcliff any more than he accounts for Rochester. He does not even account for Huntingdon in poor Anne's novel. He accounts only for himself. He is important chiefly in relation to the youngest of the Brontës. Oddly enough, this boy, who was once thought greater than his sister Emily, was curiously akin to the weak and ineffectual Anne. He shows the weird flickering of the flame that pulsed so feebly and intermittently in her. He had Anne's unhappy way with destiny, her knack of missing things. She had a touch of his morbidity. He was given to silences which in anybody but Anne would have been called morose. It was her fate to be associated with him in the hour and in the scene of his disgrace. And he was offered up unwittingly by Charlotte as a sacrifice to Anne's virtue.

* * * * *

Like Branwell, Anne had no genius. She shows for ever gentle, and, in spite of an unconquerable courage, conquered. And yet there was more in her than gentleness. There was, in this smallest and least considerable of the Brontës, an immense, a terrifying audacity. Charlotte was bold, and Emily was bolder; but this audacity of Anne's was greater than Charlotte's boldness or than Emily's, because it was willed, it was deliberate, open-eyed; it had none of the superb unconsciousness of genius. Anne took her courage in both hands when she sat down to write *The Tenant of Wildfell Hall*. There are scenes, there are situations, in Anne's amazing novel, which for sheer audacity stand alone in mid-Victorian literature, and which would hold their own in the literature of revolt that followed. It cannot be said that these scenes and situations are tackled with a master-hand. But there is a certain grasp in Anne's treatment, and an astonishing lucidity. Her knowledge of the seamy side of life was not exhaustive. But her diagnosis of certain states, her realization of certain motives, suggests Balzac rather than any of the Brontës. Thackeray, with the fear of Mrs. Grundy before his eyes, would have shrunk from recording Mrs. Huntingdon's ultimatum to her husband. The slamming of that bedroom door fairly resounds through the long emptiness of Anne's novel. But that door is the *crux* of the situation, and if Anne was not a genius she was too much of an artist to sacrifice her *crux*.

And not only was Anne revolutionary in her handling of moral situations, she was an insurgent in religious thought. Not to believe in the dogma of eternal punishment was, in mid-Victorian times and evangelical circles, to be almost an atheist. When, somewhere in the late 'seventies, Dean Farrar published his *Eternal Hope*, that book fell like a bomb into the ranks of the orthodox. But long before Dean Farrar's book Anne Brontë had thrown her bomb. There are two pages in *The Tenant of Wildfell Hall* that anticipate and sum up his now innocent arguments. Anne fairly let herself go here. And though in her "Word to the Elect" (who "may rejoice to think themselves secure") she declares that

> None shall sink to everlasting woe
> Who have not well deserved the wrath of Heaven,

she presently relents, and tacks on a poem in a lighter measure, expressing her hope

> That soon the wicked shall at last
>   Be fitted for the skies;
> And when their dreadful doom is past
>   To light and life arise.

It is said (Charlotte said it) that Anne suffered from religious melancholy of a peculiarly dark and Calvinistic type. I very much suspect that Anne's melancholy, like Branwell's passion, was pathological, and that what her soul suffered from was religious doubt. She could not reach that height where Emily moved serenely; she could not see that

> Vain are the thousand creeds
> That move men's hearts: unutterably vain.

There was a time when her tremulous, clinging faith was broken by contact with Emily's contempt for creeds. When Anne was at Haworth she and Emily were inseparable. They tramped the moors together. With their arms round each other's shoulders, they paced up and down the parlour of the Parsonage. They showed the mysterious attraction and affinity of opposites. Anne must have been fascinated, and at the same time appalled, by the radiant, revealing, annihilating sweep of Emily's thought. She was not indifferent to creeds. But you can see her fearful and reluctant youth yielding at last to Emily's thought, until she caught a glimpse of the "repose" beyond the clash of "conquered good and conquering ill". You can see how the doctrine of eternal punishment went by the board; how Anne, who had gone through agonies of orthodox fear on account of Branwell, must have adjusted things somehow, and arrived at peace. Trust in "the merits of the Redeemer" is, after all, trust in the Immensity beyond Redeemer and redeemed. Of this trust she sang in a voice, like her material voice, fragile, but sweet and true. She sang naïvely of the "Captive Dove" that makes unheard its "joyless moan", of "the heart that Nature formed to love", pining, "neglected and alone". She sang of the "Narrow Way", "Be it," she sings, "thy constant aim

> "To labour and to love,
>   To pardon and endure,
> To lift thy heart to God above,
>   And keep thy conscience pure."

She hears the wind in an alien wood and cries for the Parsonage garden, and for the "barren hills":

> Where scarce the scattered, stunted trees
>   Can yield an answering swell,
> But where a wilderness of heath
>   Returns the sound as well.
>
> For yonder garden, fair and wide,
>   With groves of evergreen,
> Long winding walks, and borders trim
>   And velvet lawns between.
>
> Restore to me that little spot,
>   With grey hills compassed round,
> Where knotted grass neglected lies,
>   And weeds usurp the ground.

For she, too, loved the moors; and through her love for them she wrote two perfect lines when she called on Memory to

> Forever hang thy dreamy spell
> Round mountain star and heather-bell.

The critics, the theorists, the tale-mongers, have left Anne quiet in that grave on the sea-coast, where she lies apart. Her gentle insignificance served her well.

*****

But no woman who ever wrote was more criticized, more spied upon, more lied about, than Charlotte. It was as if the singular purity and poverty of her legend offered irresistible provocation. The blank page called for the scribbler. The silence that hung about her was dark with challenge; it was felt to be ambiguous, enigmatic. Reserve suggests a reservation, something hidden and kept back from the insatiable public with its "right to know". Mrs. Gaskell with all her indiscretions had not given it enough. The great classic *Life of Charlotte Brontë* was, after all, incomplete. Until something more was known about her, Charlotte herself was incomplete. It was nothing that Mrs. Gaskell's work was the finest, tenderest portrait of a woman that it was ever given to a woman to achieve; nothing that she was not only recklessly and superbly loyal to Charlotte, but that in her very indiscretions she was, as far as Charlotte was concerned, incorruptibly and profoundly true.

Since Mrs. Gaskell's time, other hands have been at work on Charlotte, improving Mrs. Gaskell's masterpiece. A hundred little touches have been added to it. First, it was supposed to be too tragic, too deliberately and impossibly sombre (that sad book of which Charlotte's friend, Mary Taylor, said that it was "not so gloomy as the truth"). So first came Sir Wemyss Reid, conscientiously working up the high lights till he got the values all wrong. "If the truth must be told," he says, "the life of the author of *Jane Eyre* was by no means so joyless as the world now believes it to have been." And he sets out to give us the truth. But all that he does to lighten the gloom is to tell a pleasant story of how "one bright June morning in 1833, a handsome carriage and pair is standing opposite the 'Devonshire Arms' at Bolton

Bridge". In the handsome carriage is a young girl, Ellen Nussey, waiting for Charlotte Brontë and her brother and sisters to go with her for a picnic to Bolton Abbey.

"Presently," says Sir Wemyss Reid, "on the steep road which stretches across the moors to Keighley, the sound of wheels is heard, mingled with the merry speech and merrier laughter of fresh young voices. Shall we go forward unseen," he asks, "and study the approaching travellers whilst they are still upon the road? Their conveyance is no handsome carriage, but a rickety dog-cart, unmistakably betraying its neighbourship to the carts and ploughs of some rural farmyard. The horse, freshly taken from the fields, is driven by a youth who, in spite of his countrified dress, is no mere bumpkin. His shock of red hair hangs down in somewhat ragged locks behind his ears, for Branwell Brontë esteems himself a genius and a poet, and, following the fashion of the times, has that abhorrence of the barber's shears which genius is supposed to affect. But the lad's face is a handsome and striking one, full of Celtic fire and humour, untouched by the slightest shade of care, hopeful, promising, even brilliant. How gaily he jokes with his three sisters; with what inexhaustible volubility he pours out quotations from his favourite poets, applying them to the lovely scenes around him; and with what a mischievous delight in his superior nerve and mettle, he attempts the feats of charioteering, which fill the heart of the youngest of the party with sudden terrors! Beside him, in a dress of marvellous plainness, and ugliness, stamped with the brand "home-made" in characters which none can mistake, is the eldest of the sisters. Charlotte is talking too; there are bright smiles upon her face; she is enjoying everything around her, the splendid morning, the charms of leafy trees and budding roses, and the ever musical stream; most of all, perhaps, the charm of her brother's society, and the expectation of that coming meeting with her friends, which is so near at hand. Behind sits a pretty little girl, with fine complexion and delicate regular features, whom the stranger would pick out as the beauty of the company, and a tall, rather angular figure, clad in a dress exactly resembling Charlotte's. Emily Brontë does not talk so much as the rest of the party, but her wonderful eyes, brilliant and unfathomable as the pool at the foot of a waterfall, but radiant also with a wealth of tenderness and warmth, show how her soul is expanding under the influences of the scene; how quick she is to note the least prominent of the beauties around her, how intense is her enjoyment of the songs of the birds, the brilliancy of the sunshine, the rich scent of the flower-bespangled hedgerows. If she does not, like Charlotte and Anne, meet her brother's ceaseless flood of sparkling words with opposing currents of speech, she utters a strange, deep guttural sound which those who know her best interpret as the language of a joy too deep for articulate expression. Gaze at them as they pass you in the quiet road, and acknowledge that, in spite of their rough and even uncouth exteriors, a happier four could hardly be met with in this favourite haunt of pleasure-seekers during a long summer's day."

And you do gaze at them and are sadder, if anything, than you were before. You see them, if anything, more poignantly. You see their cheerful biographer doing all he knows, and the light he shoots across the blackness only makes it blacker.

> Nessun maggior dolore
> Che ricordarsi di tempo felice
> Nella miseria;

and in the end the biographer with all his cheerfulness succumbs to the tradition of misery, and even adds a dark contribution of his own, the suggestion of an unhappy love-affair of Charlotte's.

After Sir Wemyss Reid came Mr. Francis Grundy with *his* little pictures, *Pictures of the Past*, presenting a dreadfully unattractive Charlotte.

Then came Mr. Leyland, following Mr. Grundy, with his glorification of Branwell and his hint that Charlotte made it very hard at home for the poor boy. He repeats the story that Branwell told Mr. George Searle Phillips, how he went to see a dying girl in the village, and sat with her half an hour, and read a psalm to her and a hymn, and how he felt like praying with her too, but he was not "good enough", how he came away with a heavy heart and fell into melancholy musings. "Charlotte observed my depression," Branwell said, "and asked what ailed me. So I told her. She looked at me with a look which I shall never forget if I live to be a hundred years old—which I never shall. It was not like her at all. It wounded me as if someone had struck me a blow in the mouth. It involved ever so many things in it. It ran over me, questioning and examining, as if I had been a wild beast. It said, 'Did my ears deceive me, or did I hear aright?' And then came the painful, baffled expression, which was worse than all. It said, 'I wonder if that's true?' But, as she left the room, she seemed to accuse herself of having wronged me, and smiled kindly upon me, and said, 'She is my little scholar, and I will go and see her.' I replied not a word. I was too much cut up! When she was gone, I came over here to the 'Black Bull' and made a note of it...."

You see the implication? It was Charlotte who drove him to the "Black Bull". That was Branwell's impression of Charlotte. Just the sort of impression that an opium-eater would have of a beloved sister.

But Branwell's impression was good enough for Madame Duclaux to found her theory on. Her theory is that Charlotte was inferior to Emily in tenderness. It may well be so, and yet Charlotte would remain above most women tender, for Emily's wealth would furnish forth a score of sisters. The simple truth is that Charlotte had nerves, and Branwell was extremely trying. And it is possible that Emily had less to bear, that in her detachment she was protected more than Charlotte from Branwell at his worst.

Meanwhile tales were abroad presenting Charlotte in the queerest lights. There is that immortal story of how Thackeray gave a party for Currer Bell at his house in Young Street, and how

Currer Bell had a headache and lay on a sofa in the back drawing-room, and refused to talk to anybody but the governess; and how Thackeray at last, very late, with a finger on his lip, stole out of the house and took refuge in his club. No wonder if this quaint and curious Charlotte survived in the memory of Thackeray's daughter. But, even apart from the headache, you can see how it came about, how the sight of the governess evoked Charlotte Brontë's unforgotten agony. She saw in the amazed and cheerful lady her own sad youth, slighted and oppressed, solitary in a scene of gaiety—she could not have seen her otherwise—and her warm heart rushed out to her. She was determined that that governess should have a happy evening if nobody else had. Her behaviour was odd, if you like, it was even absurd, but it had the sublimity of vicarious expiation. Has anyone ever considered its significance, the magnitude of her deed? For Charlotte, to be the guest of honour on that brilliant night, in the house of Thackeray, her divinity, was to touch the topmost height of fame. And she turned her back on the brilliance and the fame and the face of her divinity, and offered herself up in flames as a sacrifice for all the governesses that were and had ever been and would be.

And after the fine stories came the little legends—things about Charlotte when she was a governess herself at Mrs. Sidgwick's, and the tittle-tattle of the parish. One of the three curates whom Charlotte made so shockingly immortal avenged himself for his immortality by stating that the trouble with Charlotte was that she *would* fight for mastery in the parish. Who can believe him? If there is one thing that seems more certain than another it is Charlotte's utter indifference to parochial matters. But Charlotte was just, and she may have objected to the young man's way with the Dissenters; we know that she did very strongly object to Mr. William Weightman's way. And that, I imagine, was the trouble between Charlotte and the curates.

As for the Sidgwicks, Charlotte's biographers have been rather hard on them. Mr. Leslie Stephen calls them "coarse employers". They were certainly not subtle enough to divine the hidden genius in their sad little governess. It was, I imagine, Charlotte's alien, enigmatic face that provoked a little Sidgwick to throw a Bible at her. She said Mrs. Sidgwick did not know her, and did not "intend to know her". She might have added that if she *had* intended Mrs. Sidgwick could not possibly have known her. And when the Sidgwicks said (as they did say to their cousin, Mr. Arthur Christopher Benson) that if Miss Brontë "was invited to walk to church with them, she thought she was being ordered about like a slave; if she was not invited she imagined she was being excluded from the family circle", that was simply their robust view of the paralysed attitude of a shy girl among strangers, in an agony of fear lest she should cut in where she was not wanted.

And allowances must be made for Mrs. Sidgwick. She was, no doubt, considerably annoyed at finding that she had engaged a thoroughly incompetent and apparently thoroughly morbid young person who had offered herself as a nursery-governess and didn't know how to keep order in the nursery. Naturally there was trouble at Stonegappe. Then one fine day Mrs. Sidgwick discovered that there was, after all, a use for that incomprehensible and incompetent Miss Brontë. Miss Brontë had a gift. She could sew. She could sew beautifully. Her stitching, if you would believe it, was a dream. And Mrs. Sidgwick saw that Miss Brontë's one talent was not lodged in her useless. So Charlotte sat alone all evening in the schoolroom at Stonegappe, a small figure hidden in pure white, billowy seas of muslin, and lamented thus: "She cares nothing in the world about me except to contrive how the greatest possible quantity of labour may be squeezed out of me, and to that end she overwhelms me with oceans of needlework, yards of cambric to hem, muslin night-caps to make, and above all things, dolls to dress." And Mrs. Sidgwick complained that Charlotte did not love the children, and forgot how little she liked it when the children loved Charlotte, and was unaware, poor lady, that it was recorded of her, and would be recorded to all time, that she had said, "Love the *governess*, my dear!" when her little impulsive boy put his hand in Charlotte's at the dinner-table, and cried "I love 'ou, Miss Brontë." It was the same little, impulsive boy who threw the Bible at Charlotte, and also threw a stone which hit her.

No wonder that Miss Brontë's one and only "pleasant afternoon" was when Mr. Sidgwick went out walking in his fields with his children and his Newfoundland dog, and Charlotte (by order) followed and observed him from behind.

Of course, all these old tales should have gone where Mrs. Sidgwick's old muslin caps went; but they have not, and so it has got about that Charlotte Brontë was not fond of children. Even Mr. Swinburne, at the height of his magnificent eulogy, after putting crown upon crown upon her head, pauses and wonders: had she any love for children? He finds in her "a plentiful lack of inborn baby-worship"; she is unworthy to compare in this with George Eliot, "the spiritual mother of Totty, of Eppie, and of Lillo". "The fiery-hearted Vestal of Haworth," he says, "had no room reserved in the palace of her passionate and high-minded imagination as a nursery for inmates of such divine and delicious quality." There was little Georgette in *Villette*, to say nothing of Polly, and there was Adèle in *Jane Eyre*. But Mr. Swinburne had forgotten about little Georgette. Like George Henry Lewes he is "well-nigh moved to think one of the most powerfully and exquisitely written chapters in *Shirley* a chapter which could hardly have been written at all by a woman, or, for that matter, by a man, of however noble and kindly a nature, in whom the instinct, or nerve, or organ of love for children was even of average natural strength and sensibility"; so difficult was it for him to believe in "the dread and repulsion felt by a forsaken wife and tortured mother for the very beauty and dainty sweetness of her only new-born child, as recalling the cruel, sleek charm of the human tiger that had begotten it". And so he crowns her with all crowns but that of "love for children". He is still tender to her, seeing in her that one monstrous lack; he touches it with sorrow and a certain shame.

Mr. Birrell follows him. "Miss Brontë," he says with confidence, "did not care for children. She had no eye for them. Hence it comes about that her novel-children are not good." He is moved to playful sarcasm when he tells how in August of eighteen-fifty-three "Miss Brontë suffered a keen disappointment". She went to Scotland with some friends who took their baby with them. The parents thought the baby was ill when it wasn't, and insisted on turning back, and Charlotte had to give up her holiday. "All on account of a baby," says Mr. Birrell, and refers you to Charlotte's letter on the subject, implying that it was cold-blooded. The biographer can quote letters for his purpose, and Mr. Birrell omits to tell us that Charlotte wrote "had any evil consequences followed a prolonged stay, I should never have forgiven myself". You are to imagine that Charlotte could have forgiven herself perfectly well, for Charlotte "did not care for children".

Mrs. Oliphant does not echo that cry. She was a woman and knew better.

For I believe that here we touch the very heart of the mystery that was Charlotte Brontë. We would have no right to touch it, to approach it, were it not that other people have already violated all that was most sacred and most secret in that mystery, and have given the world a defaced and disfigured Charlotte Brontë. I believe that this love of children which even Mr. Swinburne has denied to her, was the key to Charlotte's nature. We are face to face here, not with a want in her, but with an abyss, depth beyond depth of tenderness and longing and frustration, of a passion that found no clear voice in her works, because it was one with the elemental nature in her, undefined, unuttered, unutterable.

She was afraid of children; she was awkward with them; because such passion has shynesses, distances, and terrors unknown to the average comfortable women who become happy mothers. It has even its perversions, when love hardly knows itself from hate. Such love demands before all things possession. It cries out for children of its own flesh and blood. I believe that there were moments when it was pain for Charlotte to see the children born and possessed by other women. It must have been agony to have to look after them, especially when the rule was that they were not to "love the governess".

The proofs of this are slender, but they are sufficient. There is little Georgette, the sick child that Lucy nurses in the Pensionnat: "Little Georgette still piped her plaintive wail, appealing to me by her familiar term, 'Minnie, Minnie, me very poorly!' till my heart ached." ... "I affected Georgette; she was a sensitive and loving child; to hold her in my lap, or carry her in my arms, was to me a treat. To-night she would have me lay my head on the pillow of her crib; she even put her little arms round my neck. Her clasp and the nestling action with which she pressed her cheek to mine made me almost cry with a sort of tender pain."

Once during a spring-cleaning at Upperwood House Charlotte was Mrs. White's nursemaid as well as her governess, and she wrote: "By dint of nursing the fat baby it has got to know me and be fond of me. I suspect myself of growing rather fond of it." Years later she wrote to Mrs. Gaskell, after staying with her: "Could you manage to convey a small kiss to that dear but dangerous little person, Julia? She surreptitiously possessed herself of a minute fraction of my heart, which has been missing ever since I saw her."

Mrs. Gaskell tells us that there was "a strong mutual attraction" between Julia, her youngest little girl, and Charlotte Brontë. "The child," she says, "would steal her little hand into Miss Brontë's scarcely larger one, and each took pleasure in this apparently unobserved caress." May I suggest that children do not steal their little hands into the hands of people who do not care for them? Their instinct is infallible.

Charlotte Brontë tried to give an account of her feeling for children; it was something like the sacred awe of the lover. "Whenever I see Florence and Julia again I shall feel like a fond but bashful suitor, who views at a distance the fair personage to whom, in his clownish awe, he dare not risk a near approach. Such is the clearest idea I can give you of my feeling towards children I like, but to whom I am a stranger—and to what children am I not a stranger?"

Extraordinary that Charlotte's critics have missed the pathos of that *cri de coeur*. It is so clearly an echo from the "house of bondage", where Charlotte was made a stranger to the beloved, where the beloved threw stones and Bibles at her. You really have to allow for the shock of an experience so blighting. It is all part of the perversity of the fate that dogged her, that her feeling should have met with that reverse. But it was there, guarded with a certain shy austerity. She "suspected" herself of getting rather fond of the baby.

She hid her secret even from herself, as women will hide these things. But her dreams betrayed her after the way of dreams. Charlotte's dream (premonitory, she thought, of trouble) was that she carried a little crying child, and could not still its cry. "She described herself," Mrs. Gaskell says, "as having the most painful sense of pity for the little thing, lying *inert*, as sick children do, while she walked about in some gloomy place with it, such as the aisle of Haworth Church." This dream she gives to *Jane Eyre*, unconscious of its profound significance and fitness. It is a pity that Mr. Swinburne did not pay attention to Charlotte's dream.

All her life, I think, she suffered because of the perpetual insurgence of this secret, impassioned, maternal energy. Hence the sting of Lewes's famous criticism, beginning: "The grand function of woman, it must always be remembered" (as if Charlotte had forgotten it!) "is Maternity"; and, working up from his criticism of that chapter in *Shirley* to a climax of adjuration: "Currer Bell, if under your heart had ever stirred a child; if to your bosom a babe had ever been pressed—that mysterious part of your being, towards which all the rest of it was drawn, in which your whole soul was transported and absorbed—never could you have *imagined* such a falsehood as that!" It was impossible for Charlotte to protest against anything but the abominable bad taste of Lewes's article, otherwise she might have told him that she probably knew rather more about those mysteries than he did. It was she who gave us that supreme image of disastrous love. "I looked at my love; it shivered in my heart like a suffering child in a cold cradle!"

And this woman died before her child was born.

* * * * *

Then there is Mrs. Oliphant again. Though she was not one of those who said Charlotte Brontë was not fond of children, though she would have died rather than have joined Lewes in his unspeakable cry against her, Mrs. Oliphant made certain statements in no better taste than his. She suggests that Charlotte, fond or not fond of children, was too fond of matrimonial dreams. Her picture (the married woman's picture) is of an undesired and undesirable little spinster pining visibly and shamelessly in a parsonage. She would have us believe that from morning till night, from night till morning, Charlotte Brontë in the Parsonage thought of nothing but of getting married, that her dreams pursued, ruthlessly, the casual visitor. The hopelessness of the dream, the undesirability of Charlotte, is what makes her so irresistible to her sister novelist.

There was "one subject", she says, "which Charlotte Brontë had at her command, having experienced in her own person, and seen her nearest friends under the experience, of that solitude and longing of women of which she has made so remarkable an exposition. The long silence of life without an adventure or a change, the forlorn gaze out of windows which never show anyone coming who can rouse the slightest interest in the mind, the endless years and days which pass and pass, carrying away the bloom, extinguishing the lights of youth, bringing a dreary middle age before which the very soul shrinks, while yet the sufferer feels how strong is the current of life in her own veins, and how capable she is of all the active duties of existence—this was the essence and soul of the existence she knew best. Was there no help for it? Must the women wait and see their lives thrown away, and have no power to save themselves!

"The position," she goes on, "in itself so tragic, is one which can scarcely be expressed without calling forth inevitable ridicule, a laugh at the best, more often a sneer, at the women whose desire for a husband is thus betrayed. Shirley and Caroline Helstone both cried out for that husband with an indignation, a fire and impatience, a sense of wrong and injury, which stopped the laugh for the moment. It might be ludicrous, but it was horribly genuine and true." (This is more than can be said of Mrs. Oliphant's view of the adorable Shirley Keeldar who was Emily Brontë. It is ludicrous enough, and it may be genuine, but it is certainly not true.) But Mrs. Oliphant is careful not to go too far. "Note," she says, "there was nothing sensual about these young women. It was life they wanted; they knew nothing of the grosser thoughts which the world with its jeers attributes to them: of such thoughts they were unconscious in a primitive innocence which, perhaps, only women understand." Yet she characterizes their "outcry" as "indelicate". "All very well to talk of women working for their living, finding new channels for themselves, establishing their independence. How much have we said of all that" (Mrs. Oliphant thinks that she is rendering Charlotte Brontë's thought), "endeavouring to persuade ourselves! Charlotte Brontë had the courage of her opinions. It was not education nor a trade that her women wanted. It was not a living, but their share in life.... Miss Brontë herself said correct things" (observe that insincerity is insinuated here) "about the protection which a trade is to a woman, keeping her from a mercenary marriage; but this was not in the least the way of her heroines." (Why, you naturally wonder, should it have been?) "They wanted to be happy, no doubt, but above all things they wanted their share in life, to have their position by the side of men, which alone confers a natural equality, to have their shoulder to the wheel, their hands on the reins of common life, to build up the world and link the generations each to each." (And very proper of them, too.) "In her philosophy, marriage was the only state which procured this, and if she did not recommend a mercenary marriage she was at least very tolerant about its conditions, insisting less upon love than was to be expected" (!) "and with a covert conviction in her mind, that if not one man, then another was better than any complete abandonment of the larger path. Lucy Snowe for a long time had her heart very much set on Dr. John and his placid breadth of Englishism; but when she finally found out that to be impossible her tears were soon dried by the prospect of Paul Emanuel, so unlike him, coming into his place."

The obvious answer to all this is that Charlotte Brontë was writing in the mid-Victorian age, about mid-Victorian women, the women whom she saw around her; writing, without any "philosophy" or "covert conviction", in the days before emancipation, when marriage was the only chance of independence that a woman had. It would have been marvellous, if she had not had her sister Emily before her, that in such an age she should have conceived and created Shirley Keeldar. As for poor little Lucy with her two men, she is not the first heroine who mistook the false dawn for the true. Besides, Miss Brontë's "philosophy" was exactly the opposite to that attributed to her, as anybody may see who reads *Shirley*. In these matters she burned what her age adored, and adored what it burned, a thorough revolutionary.

But this is not the worst. Mrs. Oliphant professes to feel pity for her victim. "Poor Charlotte Brontë! She has not been as other women, protected by the grave from all betrayal of the episodes in her own life." (You would imagine they were awful, the episodes in Charlotte Brontë's life.) "Everybody has betrayed her, and all she thought about this one, and that, and every name that was ever associated with hers. There was a Mr. Taylor from London, about whom she wrote with great freedom to her friend, Miss Nussey, telling how the little man had come, how he had gone away without any advance in the affairs, how a chill came over her when he appeared and she found him much less attractive than when at a distance, yet how she liked it as little when he went away, and was somewhat excited about his first letter, and even went so far as to imagine with a laugh that there might possibly be a dozen little Joe Taylors before all was over."

This is atrocious. But the malice and bad taste of it are nothing to the gross carelessness and ignorance it reveals—ignorance of facts and identities and names. Charlotte's suitor was Mr. James Taylor and not Joe. Joe, the brother of her friend, Mary Taylor, was married already to a lady called Amelia, and it is of Joe and his Amelia that Charlotte writes. "She must take heart" (Amelia had been singularly unsuccessful), "there may yet be a round dozen of little Joe Taylors to look after—run after—to sort and switch and train up in the way they should go."

Of Mr. James Taylor she writes more decorously. Miss Nussey, as usual, had been thinking unwarrantable things, and had made a most unbecoming joke about Jupiter and Venus, which outraged Charlotte's "common sense". "The idea of the little man," says Charlotte, "shocks me less. He still sends his little newspaper; and the other day there came a letter of a bulk, volume, pith, judgment and knowledge, fit to have been the product of a giant. You may laugh as much and as wickedly as you please, but the fact is, there is a quiet constancy about this, my diminutive and red-haired friend, which adds a foot to his stature, turns his sandy locks dark, and altogether dignifies him a good deal in my estimation." This is all she says by way of appreciation. She says later, "His manners and his personal appearance scarcely pleased me more than at the first interview.... I feel that in his way he has a regard for me; a regard which I cannot bring myself entirely to reciprocate in kind, and yet its withdrawal leaves a painful blank." Miss Nussey evidently insists that Charlotte's feelings are engaged this time, arguing possibly from the "painful blank"; and Charlotte becomes explicit. She speaks of the disadvantages of the alleged match, and we gather that Miss Nussey has been urging her to take the little man. "But there is another thing which forms a barrier more difficult to pass than any of these. Would Mr. Taylor and I ever suit? Could I ever feel for him enough love to accept him as a husband? Friendship—gratitude—esteem I have, but each moment he came near me, and that I could see his eyes fastened on me, my veins ran ice. Now that he is away, I feel far more gently to him; it is only close by that I grow rigid—stiffening with a strange mixture of apprehension and anger—which nothing softens but his retreat, and a perfect subduing of his manner." And again, "my conscience, I can truly say, does not *now* accuse me of having treated Mr. Taylor with injustice or unkindness ... but with every disposition and with every wish, with every intention even to look on him in the most favourable point of view at his last visit, it was impossible to me in my inward heart to think of him as one that might one day be acceptable as a husband." Could anything be *more* explicit? There is a good deal more of it. After one very searching criticism of Mr. Taylor: "One does not like to say these things, but one had better be honest." And of her honesty Charlotte's letters on this subject leave no doubt. There is not the smallest ground for supposing that even for a moment had she thought of Mr. James Taylor as "one that one day might be acceptable", much less is there for Mr. Clement Shorter's suggestion that if he had come back from Bombay she would have married him.

But Joe or James, it is all one to Mrs. Oliphant, with her theory of Charlotte Brontë. "For her and her class, which did not speak of it, everything depended upon whether the women married or did not marry. Their thoughts were thus artificially fixed to one point in the horizon." The rest is repetition, ending in the astounding verdict: "The seed she thus sowed has come to many growths that would have appalled Charlotte Brontë. But while it would be very unjust to blame her for the vagaries that have followed, and to which nothing could be less desirable than any building of the house or growth of the race, any responsibility or service, we must still believe that it was she who drew the curtain first aside and opened the gates to imps of evil meaning, polluting and profaning the domestic hearth."

That is Mrs. Oliphant on Charlotte Brontë.

And even Mr. Clement Shorter, who has dealt so admirably with outrageous legends, goes half the way with the detractor. He has a theory that Charlotte Brontë was a woman of morbid mood, "to whom the problem of sex appealed with all its complications", and that she "dwelt continually on the problem of the ideal mate".

Now Charlotte may have dreamed of getting married (there have been more criminal dreams); she may have brooded continually over the problem of the ideal mate, only of all these dreams and broodings there is not one atom of evidence—not one. Not a hint, not a trace, either in her character as we know it, or in her very voluminous private correspondence. The facts of her life disprove it. Her letters to Ellen Nussey (never meant for publication) reveal the workings of Charlotte's feminine mind when applied to "the sex problem"; a mind singularly wholesome and impersonal, and singularly detached. Charlotte is full of lights upon this awful subject of matrimony, which, by the way, had considerably more interest for Miss Nussey than it had for her. In fact, if it had not been for Miss Nussey it would not have appeared so often as it did in Charlotte's letters. If you pay attention to the context (a thing that theorists never do) you see, what is indeed obvious, that a large portion of Charlotte Brontë's time was taken up in advising and controlling Ellen Nussey, that amiable and impulsive prototype of Caroline Helstone. She is called upon in all Miss Nussey's hours of crisis, and there seem to have been a great many of them. "Do not," she writes, "be over-persuaded to marry a man you can never respect—I do not say *love*, because I think if you can respect a person before marriage, moderate love at least will come after; and as to intense passion, I am convinced that that is no desirable feeling. In the first place, it seldom or never meets with a requital; and in the second place, if it did, the feeling would be only temporary; it would last the honeymoon, and then, perhaps, give place to disgust, or indifference, worse perhaps than disgust. Certainly this would be the case on the man's part; and on the woman's— God help her if she is left to love passionately and alone.

"I am tolerably well convinced that I shall never marry at all."

And again, to Miss Nussey, six months later: "Did you not once say to me in all childlike simplicity, 'I thought, Charlotte, no young lady should fall in love till the offer was actually made'? I forgot what answer I made at the time, but I now reply, after due consideration, Right as a glove, the maxim is just, and I hope you will always attend to it. I will even extend and confirm it: no young lady should fall in love till the offer has been made, accepted, the marriage ceremony performed, and the first half-year of wedded life has passed away. A woman may then begin to love, but with great precaution, very coolly, very moderately, very rationally. If she ever loves so much that a harsh word or a cold look cuts her to the heart, she is a fool. If she ever loves so much that her husband's will is her law, and that she has got into a habit of watching his looks in order that she may anticipate his wishes, she will soon be a neglected fool. Did I not tell you of an instance...?"

What could be more lucid, more light-hearted, and more sane? And if Charlotte is suspicious of the dangers of her own temperament, that only proves her lucidity and sanity the more.

Later, at Brussels, when confronted with "three or four people's" idea that "the future *époux* of Miss Brontë is on the Continent", she defends herself against the "silly imputation". "Not that it is a crime to marry, or a crime to wish to be married; but it is an imbecility, which I reject with contempt, for women, who have neither fortune nor beauty, to make marriage the principal object of their wishes and hopes, and the aim of all their actions; not to be able to convince themselves that they are unattractive, and that they had better be quiet, and think of other things than wedlock." Can anything be clearer?

So much for herself. But she has to deal with Miss Nussey, in difficulties again, later: "Papa has two or three times expressed a fear that since Mr. —— paid you so much attention, he will, perhaps, have made an impression on your mind which will interfere with your comfort. I tell him I think not, as I believe you to be mistress of yourself in those matters. Still, he keeps saying that I am to write to you and dissuade you from thinking of him. I never saw Papa make himself so uneasy about a thing of the kind before; he is usually very sarcastic on such subjects.

"Mr. —— be hanged! I never thought very well of him, and I am much disposed to think very ill of him at this blessed minute. I have discussed the subject fully, for where is the use of being mysterious and constrained?—it is not worth while."

And yet again it is Ellen Nussey. "Ten years ago I should have laughed at your account of the blunder you made in mistaking the bachelor doctor of Bridlington for a married man. I should have certainly thought you scrupulous over-much, and wondered how you could possibly regret being civil to a decent individual merely because he happened to be single instead of double. Now, however, I can perceive that your scruples are founded on common sense. I know that if women wish to escape the stigma of husband-seeking, they must act and look like marble or clay—cold, expressionless, bloodless; for every appearance of feeling, of joy, sorrow, friendliness, antipathy, admiration, disgust, are alike construed by the world into the attempt to" (I regret to say that Charlotte wrote) "to hook a husband."

Later, she has to advise her friend Mr. Williams as to a career for his daughter Louisa. And here she is miles ahead of her age, the age that considered marriage the only honourable career for a woman. "Your daughters—no more than your sons—should be a burden on your hands. Your daughters—as much as your sons—should aim at making their way honourably through life. Do you not wish to keep them at home? Believe me, teachers may be hard-worked, ill-paid and despised, but the girl who stays at home doing nothing is worse off than the hardest-wrought and worst-paid drudge of a school. Whenever I have seen, not merely in humble but in affluent houses, families of daughters sitting waiting to be married, I have pitied them from my heart. It is doubtless well—very well—if Fate decrees them a happy marriage; but, if otherwise, give their existence some object, their time some occupation, or the peevishness of disappointment, and the listlessness of idleness will infallibly degrade their nature.... Lonely as I am, how should I be if Providence had never given me courage to adopt a career...? How should I be with youth past, sisters lost, a resident in a moorland parish where there is not a single educated family? In that case I should have no world at all. As it is, something like a hope and a motive sustains me still. I wish all your daughters—I wish every woman in England, had also a hope and a motive."

Whatever the views of Charlotte Brontë's heroines may or may not have been, these were her own views—sober, sincere, and utterly dispassionate. Mrs. Oliphant set them aside, either in criminal carelessness, or with still more criminal deliberation, because they interfered with her theory. They are certainly not the views of a woman given to day-dreaming and window-gazing. Lucy Snowe may have had time for window-gazing, but not Charlotte Brontë, what with her writing and her dusting, sweeping, ironing, bed-making, and taking the eyes out of the potatoes for poor old Tabby, who was too blind to see them. Window-gazing of all things! Mrs. Oliphant could not have fixed upon a habit more absurdly at variance with Charlotte's character.

For she was pure, utterly and marvellously pure from sentimentalism, which was (and she knew it) the worst vice of the Victorian age. Mr. Leslie Stephen said that, "Miss Brontë's sense of humour was but feeble." It was robust enough when it played with sentimentalists. But as for love, for passion, she sees it with a tragic lucidity that is almost a premonition. And her attitude was by no means that of the foredoomed spinster, making necessity her virtue. There was no necessity. She had at least four suitors (quite a fair allowance for a little lady in a lonely parish), and she refused them all. Twice in her life, in her tempestuous youth, and at a crisis of her affairs, she chose "dependence upon coarse employers" before matrimony. She was shrewd, lucid, fastidious, and saw the men she knew without any glamour. To the cold but thoroughly presentable Mr. Henry Nussey she replied thus: "It has always been my habit to study the character of those among whom I chance to be thrown, and I think I know yours and can imagine what description of woman would suit you for a wife. The character should not be too marked, ardent and original, her temper should be mild, her piety undoubted, and her personal attractions sufficient to please your eyes and gratify your just pride. As for me you do not know me...." She was only three-and-twenty when she wrote that, with the prospect of Stonegappe before her. For she had not, and could not have for him, "that intense attachment which would make me willing to die for him; and if ever I marry it must be in that light of adoration that I will regard my husband". Later, in her worst loneliness she refused that ardent Mr. Taylor, who courted her by the novel means of newspapers sent with violent and unremitting regularity through the post. He represented to some degree the larger life of intellectual interest. But he offended her fastidiousness. She was sorry for the little man with his little newspaper, and that was all. She refused several times the man she ultimately married. He served a long apprenticeship to love, and Charlotte yielded to his distress rather than to her own passion. She describes her engaged state as "very calm, very expectant. What I taste of happiness is of the soberest order. I trust to love my husband. I am grateful for his tender love for me.... Providence offers me this destiny. Doubtless then it is the best for me."

These are not the words, nor is this the behaviour of Mrs. Oliphant's Charlotte Brontë, the forlorn and desperate victim of the obsession of matrimony.

I do not say that Charlotte Brontë had not what is called a "temperament"; her genius would not have been what it was without it; she herself would have been incomplete; but there never was a woman of genius who had her temperament in more complete subjection to her character; and it is her character that you have to reckon with at every turn.

The little legends and the little theories have gone far enough.

And had they gone no farther they would not have mattered much. They would at least have left Charlotte Brontë's genius to its own mystery.

But her genius was the thing that irritated, the enigmatic, inexplicable thing. Talent in a woman you can understand, there's a formula for it—*tout talent de femme est un bonheur manqué*. So when a woman's talent baffles you, your course is plain, *cherchez l'homme*. Charlotte's critics argued that if you could put your finger on the man you would have the key to the mystery. This, of course, was arguing that her genius was, after all, only a superior kind of talent; but some of them had already begun to ask themselves, Was it, after all, anything more? So they began to look for the man. They were certain by this time that there was one.

The search was difficult; for Charlotte had concealed him well. But they found him at last in M. Constantin Héger, the little Professor of the Pensionnat de Demoiselles in the Rue d'Isabelle. Sir Wemyss Reid had suggested a love-affair in Brussels to account for Charlotte's depression, which was unfavourable to his theory of the happy life. Mr. Leyland seized upon the idea, for it nourished his theory that Branwell was an innocent lamb who had never caused his sisters a moment's misery. They *made* misery for themselves out of his harmless peccadilloes. Mr. Angus Mackay in *The Brontës, Fact and Fiction*, gives us this fiction for a fact. He is pleased with what he calls the "pathetic significance" of his "discovery". There *was* somebody, there had to be, and it had to be M. Héger, for there wasn't anybody else. Mr. Mackay draws back the veil with a gesture and reveals—the love-affair. He is very nice about it, just as nice as ever he can be. "We see her," he says, "sore wounded in her affections, but unconquerable in her will. The discovery ... does not degrade the noble figure we know so well.... The moral of her greatest works—that conscience must reign absolute at whatever cost—acquires a greater force when we realize how she herself came through the furnace of temptation with marks of torture on her, but with no stain on her soul."

This is all very well, but the question is: *Did* Charlotte come through a furnace? *Did* she suffer from a great and tragic passion? It may have been so. For all we know she may have been in fifty furnaces; she may have gone from one fit of tragic passion to another. Only (apart from gossip, and apart from the argument from the novels, which begs the question) we have no evidence to prove it. What we have points all the other way.

Gossip apart, believers in the tragic passion have nourished their theory chiefly on that celebrated passage in a letter of Charlotte's to Ellen Nussey: "I returned to Brussels after Aunt's death, prompted by what then seemed an irresistible impulse. I was punished for my selfish folly by a withdrawal for more than two years of happiness and peace of mind."

Here we have the great disclosure. By "irresistible impulse" and "selfish folly", Charlotte could only mean indulgence in an illegitimate passion for M. Héger's society. Peace of mind bears but one interpretation.

Mr. Clement Shorter, to his infinite credit, will have none of this. He maintains very properly that the passage should be left to bear the simple construction that Miss Nussey and Mr. Nicholls put upon it. But I would go farther. I am convinced that not only does that passage bear that construction, but that it will not bear the weight of any other.

In eighteen-forty-two Charlotte's aunt died, and Charlotte became the head of her father's household. She left her father's house in a time of trouble, prompted by "an irresistible impulse" towards what we should now call self-development. Charlotte, more than two years later, in a moment of retrospective morbidity, called it "selfish folly". In that dark mid-Victorian age it was sin in any woman to leave her home if her home required her. And with her aunt dead, and her brother Branwell drowning his grief for his relative in drink, and her father going blind and beginning in his misery to drink a little too, Charlotte felt that her home did require her. Equally she felt that either

Emily or she had got to turn out and make a living, and since it couldn't possibly be Emily it must be she. The problem would have been quite simple even for Charlotte—but *she wanted to go.* Therefore her tender conscience vacillated. When you remember that Charlotte Brontë's conscience was, next to her genius, the largest, and at the same time the most delicate part of her, and that her love for her own people was a sacred passion, her words are sufficiently charged with meaning. A passion for M. Héger is, psychologically speaking, superfluous. You can prove anything by detaching words from their context. The letter from which that passage has been torn is an answer to Ellen Nussey's suggestions of work for Charlotte. Charlotte says "any project which infers the necessity of my leaving home is impracticable to me. If I could leave home I should not be at Haworth now. I know life is passing away, and I am doing nothing, earning nothing—a very bitter knowledge it is at moments—but I see no way out of the mist"; and so on for another line or two, and then: "These ideas sting me keenly sometimes; but whenever I consult my conscience it affirms that I am doing right in staying at home, and bitter are its upbraidings when I yield to an eager desire for release." And then, the passage quoted *ad nauseam*, to support the legend of M. Héger.

A "total withdrawal for more than two years of happiness and peace of mind". This letter is dated October 1846—more than two years since her return from Brussels in January, eighteen-forty-four. In those two years her father was threatened with total blindness, and her brother Branwell achieved his destiny. The passage refers unmistakably to events at Haworth. It is further illuminated by another passage from an earlier letter. Ellen Nussey is going through the same crisis—torn between duty to herself and duty to her people. She asks Charlotte's advice and Charlotte gives judgment: "The right path is that which necessitates the greatest sacrifice of self-interest." The sacrifice, observe, not of happiness, not of passion, but of self-interest, the development of self. It was self-development, and not passion, not happiness, that she went to Brussels for.

And Charlotte's letters from Brussels—from the scene of passion in the year of crisis, eighteen-forty-three—sufficiently reveal the nature of the trouble there. Charlotte was alone in the Pensionnat without Emily. Emily was alone at Haworth. The few friends she had in Brussels left soon after her arrival. She was alone in Brussels, and her homesickness was terrible. You can trace the malady in all its stages. In March she writes: "I ought to consider myself well off, and to be thankful for my good fortune. I hope I am thankful" (clearly she isn't thankful in the least!), "and if I could always keep up my spirits and never feel lonely or long for companionship or friendship, or whatever they call it, I should do very well." In the same letter you learn that she is giving English lessons to M. Héger and his brother-in-law, M. Chapelle. "If you could see and hear the efforts I make to teach them to pronounce like Englishmen, and their unavailing attempts to imitate, you would laugh to all eternity." Charlotte is at first amused at the noises made by M. Héger and his brother-in-law.

In May the noises made by Monsieur fail to amuse. Still, she is "indebted to him for all the pleasure or amusement" that she had, and in spite of her indebtedness, she records a "total want of companionship". "I lead an easeful, stagnant, silent life, for which … I ought to be very thankful" (but she is not). May I point out that though you may be "silent" in the first workings of a tragic and illegitimate passion, you are not "stagnant", and certainly not "easeful".

At the end of May she finds out that Madame Héger does not like her, and Monsieur is "wondrously influenced" by Madame. Monsieur has in a great measure "withdrawn the light of his countenance", but Charlotte apparently does not care. In August the *vacancies* are at hand, and everybody but Charlotte is going home. She is consequently "in low spirits; earth and heaven are dreary and empty to me at this moment".… "I can hardly write, I have such a dreary weight at my heart." But she will see it through.

She will stay some months longer "till I have acquired German". And at the end: "Everybody is abundantly civil, but homesickness comes creeping over me. I cannot shake it off." That was in September, in M. Héger's absence. Later, she tells Emily how she went into the cathedral and made "a real confession *to see what it was like*". Charlotte's confession has been used to bolster up the theory of the "temptation". Unfortunately for the theory it happened in September, when M. Héger and temptation were not there. In October she finds that she no longer trusts Madame Héger. At the same time "solitude oppresses me to an excess". She gave notice, and M. Héger flew into a passion and commanded her to stay. She stayed very much against, not her conscience, but her will. In the same letter and the same connection she says, "I have much to say—many little odd things, queer and puzzling enough—which I do not like to trust to a letter, but which one day perhaps, or rather one evening—if ever we should find ourselves by the fireside at Haworth or Brookroyd, with our feet on the fender curling our hair—I may communicate to you."

Charlotte is now aware of a situation; she is interested in it, intellectually, not emotionally.

In November: "Twinges of homesickness cut me to the heart, now and then." On holidays "the silence and loneliness of all the house weighs down one's spirits like lead.... Madame Héger, good and kind as I have described her" (*i.e.* for all her goodness and kindness), "never comes near me on these occasions." ... "She is not colder to me than she is to the other teachers, but they are less dependent on her than I am." But the situation is becoming clearer. Charlotte is interested. "I fancy I begin to perceive the reason of this mighty distance and reserve; it sometimes makes me laugh, and at other times nearly cry. When I am sure of it I will tell you."

There can be no doubt that before she left Brussels Charlotte was sure; but there is no record of her ever having told.

The evidence from the letters is plain enough. But the first thing that the theorist does is to mutilate letters. He suppresses all those parts of a correspondence which tell against his theory. When these torn and bleeding passages are restored piously to their contexts they are destructive to the legend of tragic passion. They show (as Mr. Clement Shorter has pointed out) that throughout her last year at Brussels Charlotte Brontë saw hardly anything of M. Héger. They also show that before very long Charlotte had a shrewd suspicion that Madame had arranged it so, and that it was not so much the absence of Monsieur that disturbed her as the extraordinary behaviour of Madame. And they show that from first to last she was incurably homesick.

Now if Charlotte had been in any degree, latently, or increasingly, or violently in love with M. Héger, she would have been as miserable as you like in M. Héger's house, but she would not have been homesick; she would not, I think, have worried quite so much about Madame's behaviour; and she would have found the clue to it sooner than she did.

To me it is all so simple and self-evident that, if the story were not revived periodically, if it had not been raked up again only the other day,[A] there would be no need to dwell upon anything so pitiful and silly.

[Footnote A: See *The Key to the Brontë Works*, by J. Malham-Dembleby, 1911.]

It rests first and foremost on gossip, silly, pitiful gossip and conjecture. Gossip in England, gossip in Brussels, conjecture all round. Above all, it rests on certain feline hints supplied by Madame Héger and her family. Charlotte's friends were always playfully suspecting her of love-affairs. They could never put their fingers on the man, and they missed M. Héger. It would never have occurred to their innocent mid-Victorian minds to suspect Charlotte of an attachment to a married man. It would not have occurred to Charlotte to suspect herself of it. But Madame Héger was a Frenchwoman, and she had not a mid-Victorian mind, and she certainly suspected Charlotte of an attachment, a flagrant attachment, to M. Héger. It is well known that Madame made statements to that effect, and it is admitted on all hands that Madame had been jealous. It may fairly be conjectured that it was M. Héger and not Charlotte who gave her cause, slight enough in all conscience, but sufficient for Madame Héger. She did not understand these Platonic relations between English teachers and their French professors. She had never desired Platonic relations with anybody herself, and she saw nothing but annoyance in them for everybody concerned. Madame's attitude is the clue to the mystery, the clue that Charlotte found. She accused the dead Charlotte of an absurd and futile passion for her husband; she stated that she had had to advise the living Charlotte to moderate the ardour of her admiration for the engaging professor; but the truth, as Charlotte in the end discovered, was that for a certain brief period Madame was preposterously jealous. M. Héger confessed as much when he asked Charlotte to address her letters to him at the Athénée Royale instead of the Pensionnat. The correspondence, he said, was disagreeable to his wife.

Why, in Heaven's name, disagreeable, if Madame Héger suspected Charlotte of an absurd and futile passion? And why should Madame Héger have been jealous of an absurd and futile woman, a woman who had seen so little of Madame Héger's husband, and who was then in England? I cannot agree with Mr. Shorter that M. Héger regarded Charlotte with indifference. He was a Frenchman, and he had his vanity, and no doubt the frank admiration of his brilliant pupil appealed to it vividly in moments of conjugal depression. Charlotte herself must have had some attraction for M. Héger. Madame perceived the appeal and the attraction, and she was jealous; therefore her interpretation of appearances could not have been so unflattering to Charlotte as she made out. Madame, in fact, suspected, on her husband's part, the dawning of an attachment. We know nothing about M. Héger's attachment, and we haven't any earthly right to know; but from all that is known of M. Héger it is certain that, if it was not entirely intellectual, not entirely that "*affection presque paternelle*" that he once professed, it was entirely restrained and innocent and honourable. It is Madame Héger with her jealousy who has given the poor gentleman away. Monsieur's state of mind—extremely temporary—probably accounted for "those many odd little things, queer and puzzling enough", which Charlotte would not trust to a letter; matter for curl-paper confidences and no more.

Of course there is the argument from the novels, from *The Professor*, from *Jane Eyre*, from *Villette*. I have not forgotten it. But really it begs the question. It moves in an extremely narrow and an extremely vicious circle. Jane Eyre was tried in a furnace of temptation, therefore Charlotte must have been tried. Lucy Snowe and Frances Henri loved and suffered in Brussels. Therefore Charlotte must have loved and suffered there. And if Charlotte loved and suffered and was tried in a furnace of temptation, that would account for Frances and for Lucy and for Jane.

No; the theorists who have insisted on this tragic passion have not reckoned with Charlotte Brontë's character, and its tremendous power of self-repression. If at Brussels any disastrous tenderness had raised its head it wouldn't have had a chance to grow an inch. But Charlotte had large and luminous ideas of friendship. She was pure, utterly pure from all the illusions and subtleties and corruptions of the sentimentalist, and she could trust herself in friendship. She brought to it ardours and vehemences that she would never have allowed to love. If she let herself go in her infrequent intercourse with M. Héger, it was because she was so far from feeling in herself the possibility of passion. That was why she could say, "I think, however long I live, I shall not forget what the parting with M. Héger cost me. It grieved me so much to grieve him who has been so true, kind, and disinterested a friend." That was how she could bring herself to write thus to Monsieur: "*Savez-vous ce que je ferais, Monsieur? J'écrirais un livre et je le dédierais à mon maître de littérature, au seul maître que j'aie jamais eu—à vous Monsieur! Je vous ai dit souvent en français combien je vous respecte, combien je suis redevable à votre bonté à vos conseils. Je voudrais le dire une fois en anglais ... le souvenir de vos bontés ne s'effacera jamais de ma mémoire, et tant que ce souvenir durera le respect que vous m'avez inspiré durera aussi.*" For "*je vous respecte*" we are not entitled to read "*je vous aime*". Charlotte was so made that kindness shown her moved her to tears of gratitude. When Charlotte said "respect" she meant it. Her feeling for M. Héger was purely what Mr. Matthew Arnold said religion was, an affair of "morality touched with emotion". All her utterances, where there is any feeling in them, no matter what, have a poignancy, a vibration which is Brontësque and nothing more. And this Brontësque quality is what the theorists have (like Madame Héger, and possibly Monsieur) neither allowed for nor understood.

* * * * *

For this "fiery-hearted Vestal", this virgin, sharp-tongued and sharper-eyed, this scorner of amorous curates, had a genius for friendship. This genius, like her other genius, was narrow in its range and opportunity, and for that all the more ardent and intense. It fed on what came to its hand. It could even grow, like her other genius, with astounding vitality out of strange and hostile soil. She seems to have had many friends, obscure and great; the obscure, the Dixons, the Wheelrights, the Taylors, the Nusseys, out of all proportion to the great. But properly speaking she had only two friends, Mary Taylor and Ellen Nussey, the enchanting, immortal "Nel".

There *is* something at first sight strange and hostile about Mary Taylor, the energetic, practical, determined, terribly robust person you see so plainly trying, in the dawn of their acquaintance, to knock the nonsense out of Charlotte. Mary Taylor had no appreciation of the Brontësque. When Charlotte told Mary Taylor that at Cowan Bridge she used to stand in the burn on a stone to watch the water flow by, Mary Taylor told Charlotte that she should have gone fishing. When *Jane Eyre* appeared she wrote to Charlotte in a strain that is amusing to posterity. There is a touch of condescension in her praise. She is evidently surprised at anything so great coming out of Charlotte. "It seemed to me incredible that you had actually written a book." "You are very different from me," she says, "in having no doctrine to preach. It is impossible to squeeze a moral out of your production." She is thinking of his prototype when she criticizes the character of St. John Rivers. "A missionary either goes into his office for a piece of bread, or he goes for enthusiasm, and that is both too good and too bad a quality for St. John. It's a bit of your absurd charity to believe in such a man." As an intellectual woman Mary Taylor realized Charlotte Brontë's intellect, but it is doubtful if she ever fully realized what, beyond an intellect, she had got hold of in her friend. She was a woman of larger brain than Ellen Nussey, she was loyal and warm-hearted to the last degree, but it was not given to her to see in Charlotte Brontë what Ellen Nussey, little as you would have expected it, had seen. She did not keep her letters. She burnt them "in a fit of caution", which may have been just as well.

But Mary Taylor is important. She had, among her more tender qualities, an appalling frankness. It was she who told poor little Charlotte that she was very ugly. Charlotte never forgot it. You can feel in her letters, in her novels, in her whole nature, the long reverberation of the shock. She said afterwards: "You did me a great deal of good, Polly," by which she meant that Polly had done her an infinity of harm.

Her friends all began by trying to do her good. Even Ellen Nussey tried. Charlotte is very kindly cautioned against being "tempted by the fondness of my sisters to consider myself of too much importance", and in a parenthesis Ellen Nussey begs her not to be offended. "Oh, Ellen," Charlotte writes, "do you think I could be offended by any good advice you may give me?" She thanks her heartily, and loves her "if possible all the better for it". Ellen Nussey in her turn asks Charlotte to tell her of her faults and "cease flattering her". Charlotte very sensibly refuses; and it is not till she has got away from her sisters that her own heart-searchings begin. They are mainly tiresome, but there is a flash of revelation in her reply to "the note you sent me with the umbrella". "My darling, if I were like you, I should have to face Zionwards, though prejudice and error might occasionally fling a mist over the glorious vision before me, for with all your single-hearted sincerity you have your faults, but *I* am not like you. If you knew my thoughts; the dreams that absorb me, and the fiery imagination that at times eats me up, and makes me feel society, as it is, wretchedly insipid, you would pity me, and I dare say despise me." Miss Nussey writes again, and Charlotte trembles "all over with excitement" after reading her note. "I will no longer shrink from your question," she replies. "I *do* wish to be better than I am. I pray fervently sometimes to be made so ... this very night I will pray as you wish me."

But Charlotte is not in the least like Ellen Nussey, and she still refuses to be drawn into any return of this dangerous play with a friend's conscience and her nerves. "I will not tell you all I think and feel about you, Ellen. I will preserve unbroken that reserve which alone enables me to maintain a decent character for judgment; but for that, I should long ago have been set down by all who knows me as a Frenchified fool. You have been very kind to me of late, and gentle, and you have spared me those little sallies of ridicule, which, owing to my miserable and wretched touchiness of character, used formerly to make me wince, as if I had been touched with hot iron. Things that nobody else cares for enter into my mind and rankle there like venom. I know these feelings are absurd, and therefore I try to hide them, but they only sting the deeper for concealment. I'm an idiot!"

Miss Nussey seems to have preserved her calm through all the excitement and to have never turned a hair. But nothing could have been worse for Charlotte than this sort of thing. It goes on for years. It began in eighteen-thirty-three, the third year of their friendship, when she was seventeen. In 'thirty-seven it is at its height. Charlotte writes from Dewsbury Moor: "If I could always live with you, if your lips and mine could at the same time drink the same draught at the same pure fountain of mercy, I hope, I trust, I might one day become better, far better than my evil, wandering thoughts, my corrupt heart, cold to the spirit and warm to the flesh, will now permit me to be. I often plan the pleasant life we might lead, strengthening each other in the power of self-denial, that hallowed and glowing devotion which the past Saints of God often attained to."

Now a curious and interesting thing is revealed by this correspondence. These religious fervours and depressions come on the moment Charlotte leaves Haworth and disappear as soon as she returns. All those letters were written from Roe Head or Dewsbury Moor, while the Haworth letters of the same period are sane and light-hearted. And when she is fairly settled at Haworth, instead of emulating the Saints of God, she and Miss Nussey are studying human nature and the art of flirtation as exhibited by curates. Charlotte administers to her friend a formidable amount of worldly wisdom, thus avenging herself for the dance Miss Nussey led her round the throne of grace.

For, though that morbid excitement and introspection belonged solely to Charlotte's days of exile, Miss Nussey was at the bottom of it. Mary Taylor would have been a far robuster influence. But Charlotte's friendship for Mary Taylor, warm as it was, strikes cold beside her passionate affection for Ellen Nussey. She brought her own fire to that, and her own extraordinary capacity for pain. Her letters show every phase of this friendship, its birth, its unfolding; and then the sudden leaping of the flame, its writhing and its torture. She writes with a lover's ardour and impatience. "Write to me very soon and dispel my uncertainty, or I shall get impatient, almost irritable." "I read your letter with dismay. Ellen—what shall I do without you? Why are we to be denied each other's society? It is an inscrutable fatality.... Why are we to be divided?" (She is at Roe Head, and Roe Head suggests the answer.) "Surely, Ellen, it must be because we are in danger of loving each other too well—of losing sight of the *Creator* in idolatry of the *creature*." She prays to be resigned, and records "a sweet, placid sensation like those that I remember used to visit me when I was a little child, and on Sunday evenings in summer stood by the window reading the life of a certain French nobleman who attained a purer and higher degree of sanctity than has been known since the days of the Early Martyrs. I thought of my own Ellen—" "I wish I could see you, my darling; I have lavished the warmest affections of a very hot tenacious heart upon you; if you grow cold, it is over." She was only twenty-one.

A few more years and the leaping and the writhing and the torture cease, the fire burns to a steady, inextinguishable glow. There is gaiety in Charlotte's tenderness. She is "infuriated" on finding a jar in her trunk. "At first I hoped it was empty, but when I found it heavy and replete, I could have hurled it all the way back to Birstall. However, the inscription A.B. softened me much. You ought first to be tenderly kissed, and then as tenderly whipped. Emily is just now sitting on the floor of the bedroom where I am writing, looking at her apples. She smiled when I gave them and the collar as your presents, with an expression at once well pleased and slightly surprised."

The religious fervours and the soul-searchings have ceased long ago, so has Miss Nussey's brief spiritual ascendency. But the friendship and the letters never cease. They go on for twenty years, through exile and suffering, through bereavement, through fame and through marriage, uninterrupted and, except for one brief period, unabridged. There is nothing in any biography to compare with those letters to Ellen Nussey. If Charlotte Brontë had not happened to be a great genius as well as a great woman, they alone would have furnished forth her complete biography. There is no important detail of her mere life that is not given in them. Mrs. Gaskell relied almost entirely on them, and on information supplied to her by Miss Nussey. And each critic and biographer who followed her, from Sir Wemyss Reid to Mr. Clement Shorter, drew from the same source. Miss Nussey was

almost the only safe repository of material relating to Charlotte
Brontë. She had possessed hundreds of her letters and, with that
amiable weakness which was the defect of her charming quality,
she was unable to withhold any of them from the importunate
researcher. There seems to have been nothing, except one thing,
that Charlotte did not talk about to Miss Nussey when they sat
with their feet on the fender and their hair in curl-papers. That
one thing was her writing. It is quite possible that in those curl-
paper confidences Miss Nussey learnt the truth about Charlotte's
friend, M. Héger. She never learnt anything about Charlotte's
genius. In everything that concerned her genius Charlotte was
silent and secret with her friend. That was the line, the very sharp
and impassable line she drew between her "dear, *dear* Ellen", her
"dearest Nel", and her sisters, Anne and Emily. The freemasonry
of friendship ended there. You may search in vain through
even her later correspondence with Miss Nussey for any more
than perfunctory and extraneous allusions to her works. It
was as if they had never been. Every detail of her daily life is
there, the outer and the inner things, the sewing and ironing
and potato-peeling, together with matters of the heart and soul,
searchings, experiences, agonies; the figures of her father, her
brother, her sisters, move there, vivid and alive; and old Tabby
and the curates; and the very animals, Keeper and Flossie, and
the little black cat, Tom, that died and made Emily sorry; but of
the one thing not a word. The letters to Ellen Nussey following
the publication of *Jane Eyre* are all full of gossip about Miss
Ringrose and the Robinsons. Presently Ellen hears a rumour of
publication. Charlotte repudiates it and friction follows.

 Charlotte writes: "Dear Ellen,—write another letter and explain
that note of yours distinctly.... Let me know what you heard, and
from whom you heard it. You do wrong to feel pain from any
circumstance, or to suppose yourself slighted...." "Dear Ellen,—
All I can say to you about a certain matter is this: the report
... must have had its origin in some absurd misunderstanding.
I have given *no one* a right to affirm or hint in the most distant

manner that I am publishing (humbug!). Whoever has said it—if anyone has, which I doubt—is no friend of mine. Though twenty books were ascribed to me, I should own none. I scout the idea utterly. Whoever, after I have distinctly rejected the charge, urges it upon me, will do an unkind and ill-bred thing." If Miss Nussey is asked, she is authorized by Miss Brontë to say, "that she repels and disowns every accusation of the kind. You may add, if you please, that if anyone has her confidence, you believe you have, and she has made no drivelling confessions to you on that subject." "Dear Ellen,—I shall begin by telling you that you have no right to be angry at the length of time I have suffered to slip by since receiving your last, without answering it; because you have often kept me waiting much longer, and having made this gracious speech, thereby obviating reproaches, I will add that I think it a great shame, when you receive a long and thoroughly interesting letter, full of the sort of details you fully relish, to read the same with selfish pleasure, and not even have the manners to thank your correspondent, and express how very much you enjoyed the narrative. I *did* enjoy the narrative in your last very keenly.... Which of the Miss Woolers did you see at Mr. Allbutts?"

A beautiful but most unequal friendship. "The sort of details you fully relish—" How that phrase must have rankled! You can hear the passionate protest: "Those details are not what I relish in the least. Putting me off with your Woolers and your Allbutts! If only you had told me about *Jane Eyre*!" For it turned out that all the time Mary Taylor had been told. The inference was that Mary Taylor, with her fits of caution, could be trusted.

This silence of Charlotte's must have been most painful and incomprehensible to the poor Ellen who was Caroline Helstone. She had been the first to divine Charlotte's secret; for she kept the letters. She must have felt like some tender and worshipping wife to whom all doors in the house of the beloved are thrown open, except the door of the sanctuary, which is persistently slammed in her charming face. There must have come to her moments of terrible insight when she felt the danger and the mystery of the flaming spirit she had tried to hold. But Charlotte's friend can wear her half-pathetic immortality with grace. She could at least say: "She told me things she never told anyone else. I have hundreds of her letters. And I had her heart."

* * * * *

Nothing so much as this correspondence reveals the appalling solitude in which the Brontës lived. Here is their dearest and most intimate friend, and she is one to whom they can never speak of the thing that interested them most. No doubt "our best plays mean secret plays"; but Charlotte, at any rate, suffered from this secrecy. There was nothing to counteract Miss Nussey's direful influence on her spiritual youth. "Papa" highly approved of the friendship. He wished it to continue, and it did; and it was the best that Charlotte had. I know few things more pathetic than the cry that Charlotte, at twenty-one, sent out of her solitude (with some verses) to Southey and to Wordsworth. Southey told her that, "Literature cannot be the business of a woman's life, and it ought not to be. The more she is engaged in her proper duties, the less leisure will she have for it, even as an accomplishment and a recreation. To those duties you have not yet been called, and when you are you will be less eager for celebrity." A sound, respectable, bourgeois opinion so far, but Southey went farther. "Write poetry for its own sake," he said; and he could hardly have said better. Charlotte treasured the letter, and wrote on the cover of it, "Southey's advice, to be kept for ever." Wordsworth's advice, I am sorry to say, provoked her to flippancy.

And that, out of the solitude, was all. Not the ghost, not the shadow of an Influence came to the three sisters. There never was genius that owed so little to influence as theirs.

I know that in Charlotte's case there is said to have been an Influence. An Influence without which she would have remained for ever in obscurity, with *Villette*, with *Shirley*, with *Jane Eyre*, with *The Professor*, unborn, unconceived.

Need I say that the Influence is—M. Héger?

"The sojourn in Brussels," says Mr. Clement Shorter, "made Miss Brontë an author," and he is only following Sir Wemyss Reid, who was the first to establish Brussels as the turning-point. Mr. Shorter does not believe in M. Héger as the inspirer of passion, but he does believe in him as the inspirer of genius. He thinks it exceedingly probable that had not circumstances led Charlotte Brontë to spend some time at Brussels not only would "the world never have heard of her", but it would never have heard of her sisters. He is quite certain about Charlotte anyhow; she could not have "arrived" had she not met M. Héger. "She went," he says, "to Brussels full of the crude ambitions, the semi-literary impulses that are so common on the fringe of the writing world. She left Brussels a woman of genuine cultivation, of educated tastes, armed with just the equipment that was to enable her to write the books of which two generations of her countrymen have been justly proud."

This is saying that Charlotte Brontë had no means of expression before she wrote *devoirs* under M. Héger. True, her genius did not find itself until after she left Brussels, that is to say, not until she was nearly thirty. I have not read any of her works as Lord Charles Albert Florian Wellesley, and I do not imagine they were works of genius. But that only means that Charlotte Brontë's genius took time. She was one of those novelists who do not write novels before they are nearly thirty. But she could write. Certain fragments of her very earliest work show that from the first she had not only the means, but very considerable mastery of expression. What is more, they reveal in germ the qualities that marked her style in its maturity. Her styles rather, for she had several. There is her absolutely simple style, in which she is perfect; her didactic style, her fantastic style, which are mere temporary aberrations; and her inspired style, in which at her worst she is merely flamboyant and redundant, and at her best no less than perfect. You will find a faint, embryonic foreshadowing of her perfections in the fragments given by Mrs. Gaskell. There is THE HISTORY OF THE YEAR 1829, beginning: "Once Papa lent my sister Maria a book. It was an old geography book; she wrote on its blank leaf, "Papa lent me this book." This book is a hundred and twenty years old; it is at this moment lying before me. While I write this I am in the kitchen of the Parsonage, Haworth; Tabby, the servant, is washing up the breakfast things, and Anne, my youngest sister (Maria was my eldest), is kneeling on a chair, looking at some cakes, which Tabby has been baking for us." You cannot beat that for pure simplicity of statement. There is another fragment that might have come straight out of *Jane Eyre*. "One night, about the time when the cold sleet and stormy fogs of November are succeeded by the snowstorms and high piercing night-winds of confirmed winter, we were all sitting round the warm, blazing kitchen fire, having just concluded a quarrel with Tabby concerning the propriety of lighting a candle, from which she came off victorious, no candle having been produced." And there is a dream-story that Mr. Clement Shorter gives. She is in the "Mines of Cracone", under the floor of the sea. "But in the midst of all this magnificence I felt an indescribable sense of fear and terror, for the sea raged above us, and by the awful and tumultuous noises of roaring winds and dashing waves, it seemed as if the storm was violent. And now the massy pillars groaned beneath the pressure of the ocean, and the glittering arches seemed about to be overwhelmed. When I heard the rushing waters and saw a mighty flood rolling towards me I gave a loud shriek of terror." The dream changes: she is in a desert full of barren rocks and high mountains, where she sees "by the light of his own fiery eyes a royal lion rousing himself from his kingly slumbers. His terrible eye was fixed upon me, and the desert rang, and the rocks echoed with the tremendous roar of fierce delight which he uttered as he sprang towards me." And there is her letter to the editor of one of their *Little Magazines*: "Sir,—It is well known that the Genii have declared that unless they perform certain arduous duties every year, of a mysterious nature, all the worlds in the firmament will be burnt up, and gathered together in one mighty globe, which will roll in solitary splendour through the vast wilderness of space, inhabited only by the four high princes of the Genii, till time shall be succeeded by Eternity; and the impudence of this is only to be paralleled by another of their assertions, namely, that by their magic might they can reduce the world to a desert, the purest waters to streams of livid poison, and the clearest lakes to stagnant water, the pestilential vapours of which shall slay all living creatures, except the bloodthirsty beast of the forest, and the ravenous bird of the rock. But that in the midst of this desolation the palace of the chief Genii shall rise sparkling in the wilderness, and the horrible howl of their war-cry shall spread over the land at morning, at noontide, and at night; but that they shall have their annual feast over the bones of the dead, and shall yearly rejoice with the joy of victors. I think, sir, that the horrible wickedness of this needs no remark, and therefore I hasten to subscribe myself, etc."

Puerile, if you like, and puerile all the stuff that Charlotte Brontë wrote before eighteen-forty-six; but her style at thirteen, in its very rhythms and cadences, is the unmistakable embryo of her style at thirty; and M. Héger no more cured her of its faults that he could teach her its splendours. Something that was not Brussels made Miss Brontë a prodigious author at thirteen. The mere mass of her *Juvenilia* testifies to a most ungovernable bent. Read the list of works, appalling in their length, which this child produced in a period of fifteen months; consider that she produced nothing but melancholy letters during her "sojourn in Brussels"; and compare M. Héger's academic precepts with her practice, with the wild sweep and exuberance of her style when she has shaken him off, and her genius gets possession of her.

I know there is a gulf fixed between Currer Bell and Charles Townsend, who succeeded Lord Charles Albert Florian Wellesley and the Marquis of Douro, about eighteen-thirty-eight; but it is bridged by the later *Poems* which show Charlotte's genius struggling through a wrong medium to the right goal. She does not know—after the sojourn in Brussels she does not yet know—that her right medium is prose. She knew no more than she knew in November, eighteen-forty-one, when, on the eve of her flight from Haworth, she writes: "The plain fact is, I was not, I am not now, certain of my destiny." It was not until two years after she had returned to Haworth that she received her certainty. For posterity, overpowered by the labour of the Brontë specialists, it may seem as if Charlotte Brontë's genius owed everything to her flight from Haworth. In reality her flight merely coincided with the inevitable shooting of its wings; and the specialists have mistaken coincidence for destiny.

Heaven only knows what would have happened to her genius if, blind to her destiny, she had remained in Brussels. For, once there, its wing-feathers left off growing. Its way was blocked by every conceivable hostile and obstructive thing. Madame Héger was hostile, and Monsieur, I think, purely obstructive. Emily saw through him, and denounced his method as fatal to all originality. Charlotte, to be sure, called him "my dear master, the only master that I ever had", but if that was not her "absurd charity", it was only her Brontësque way. There was no sense in which he was her master. He taught her French; to the very last the habit of using "a few French words" was the King Charles's head in her manuscripts; and the French he taught her did her harm. The restraint he could and would have taught her she never learnt until her genius had had, in defiance and in spite of him, its full fling.

And what a fling! It is the way of genius to look after itself. In spite of obstacles, Charlotte Brontë's took hold of every man and woman that crossed and barred its path, and ultimately it avenged itself on Monsieur and on Madame Héger. Those two were made for peaceful, honourable conjugal obscurity, but it was their luck to harbour a half-fledged and obstructed genius in their Pensionnat, a genius thirsting for experience; and somehow, between them, they contrived to make it suffer. That was their tragedy. Monsieur's case is pitiful; for he was kind and well-meaning, and he was fond of Charlotte; and yet, because of Charlotte, there is no peace for him in the place where he has gone. Her genius has done with him, but her ghost, like some malign and awful destiny, pursues him. No sooner does he sink back quiet in his grave than somebody unearths him. Why cannot he be allowed to rest, once for all, in his amiable unimportance? He became, poor man, important only by the use that Charlotte's genius made of him. It seized him as it would have seized on any other interesting material that came its way. Without him we might have had another Rochester, and we should not have had any Paul Emanuel, which would have been a pity; that is all.

There is hardly any hope that Brontë specialists will accept this view. For them the sojourn in Brussels will still stand as the turning-point in Charlotte Brontë's career. Yet for her, long afterwards, Brussels must have stood as the danger threatening it. She would have said, I think, that her sojourn in Haworth was the turning-point. It was destiny that turned Emily back to Haworth from the destruction that waited for her at Brussels, so that she conceived and brought forth *Wuthering Heights*; her own destiny that she secretly foreknew, consoling and beneficent. And, no doubt, it was destiny of a sort, unforeknown, deceitful, apparently malignant, that sent Charlotte back again to Brussels after her aunt's death. It wrung from her her greatest book, *Villette*. But Haworth, I think, would have wrung from her another and perhaps a greater.

For the first-fruits of the sojourn in Brussels was neither *Villette* nor *Jane Eyre*, but *The Professor*. And *The Professor* has none of the qualities of *Jane Eyre* or of *Villette*; it has none of the qualities of Charlotte's later work at all; above all, none of that master quality which M. Héger is supposed to have specially evoked. Charlotte, indeed, could not well have written a book more destructive to the legend of the upheaval, the tragic passion, the furnace of temptation and the flight. Nothing could be less like a furnace than the atmosphere of *The Professor*. From the first page to the last there is not one pulse, not one breath of passion in it. The bloodless thing comes coldly, slowly tentatively, from the birth. It is almost as frigid as a *devoir* written under M. Héger's eye. The theorists, I notice, are careful not to draw attention to *The Professor*; and they are wise, for attention drawn to *The Professor* makes sad work of their theory.

Remember, on the theory, Charlotte Brontë has received her great awakening, her great enlightenment; she is primed with passion; the whole wonderful material of *Villette* is in her hand; she has before her her unique opportunity. You ought, on the theory, to see her hastening to it, a passionate woman, pouring out her own one and supreme experience, and, with the brand of Brussels on her, never afterwards really doing anything else. Whereas the first thing the impassioned Charlotte does (after a year of uninspired and ineffectual poetizing) is to sit down and write *The Professor*; a book, remarkable not by any means for its emotion, but for its cold and dispassionate observation. Charlotte eliminates herself, and is Crimsworth in order that she may observe Frances Henri the more dispassionately. She is inspired solely by the analytic spirit, and either cannot, or will not, let herself go. But she does what she meant to do. She had it in mind to write, not a great work of imagination, but a grey and sober book, and a grey and sober book is what she writes. A book concerned only with things and people she has seen and known; a book, therefore, from which passion and the poetry that passion is must be rigidly excluded, as belonging to the region of things not, strictly speaking, known. It is as if she had written *The Professor* in rivalry with her sister Anne, both of them austerely determined to put aside all imagination and deal with experience and experience alone. Thus you obtain sincerity, you obtain truth. And with nothing but experience before her, she writes a book that has no passion in it, a book almost as bloodless and as gentle as her sister Anne's.

Let us not disparage *The Professor*. Charlotte herself did not disparage it. In her Preface she refused to solicit "indulgence for it on the plea of a first attempt. A first attempt," she says, "it certainly was not, as the pen which wrote it had been previously worn in a practice of some years." In that Preface she shows plainly that at the very outset of her career she had no sterner critic than herself; that she was aware of her sins and her temptations, and of the dangers that lurked for her in her imaginative style. "In many a crude effort, destroyed almost as soon as composed, I had got over any such taste as I might have had for ornamented and decorated composition, and come to prefer what was plain and homely." Observe, it is not to the lessons of the "master", but to the creation and destruction that went on at Haworth that she attributes this purgation. She is not aware of the extent to which she can trust her genius, of what will happen when she has fairly let herself go. She is working on a method that rules her choice of subject. "I said to myself that my hero should work his way through life, as I had seen real, living men work theirs—that he should never get a shilling that he had not earned—that no sudden turns should lift him in a moment to wealth and high station; that whatever small competency he might gain should be won by the sweat of his brow; that before he could find so much as an arbour to sit down in, he should master at least half the ascent of the Hill Difficulty; that he should not marry even a beautiful girl or a lady of rank."

There was no fine madness in that method; but its very soundness and sanity show the admirable spirit in which Charlotte Brontë approached her art. She was to return to the method of *The Professor* again and yet again, when she suspected herself of having given imagination too loose a rein. The remarkable thing was that she should have begun with it.

And in some respects *The Professor* is more finished, better constructed than any of her later books. There is virtue in its extreme sobriety. Nothing could be more delicate and firm than the drawing of Frances Henri; nothing in its grey style more admirable than the scene where Crimsworth, having found Frances in the cemetery, takes her to her home in the Rue Notre

Dame aux Neiges.

"Stepping over a little mat of green wool, I found myself in a small room with a painted floor and a square of green carpet in the middle; the articles of furniture were few, but all bright and exquisitely clean—order reigned through its narrow limits—such order as it suited my punctilious soul to behold.... Poor the place might be; poor truly it was, but its neatness was better than elegance, and had but a bright little fire shone on that clean hearth, I should have deemed it more attractive than a palace. No fire was there, however, and no fuel laid ready to light; the lace-mender was unable to allow herself that indulgence.... Frances went into an inner room to take off her bonnet, and she came out a model of frugal neatness, with her well-fitting black stuff dress, so accurately defining her elegant bust and taper waist, with her spotless white collar turned back from a fair and shapely neck, with her plenteous brown hair arranged in smooth bands on her temples and in a large Grecian plait behind: ornaments she had none—neither brooch, ring, nor ribbon; she did well enough without them—perfection of fit, proportion of form, grace of carriage, agreeably supplied their place." Frances lights a fire, having fetched wood and coal in a basket.

"'It is her whole stock, and she will exhaust it out of hospitality,' thought I.

"'What are you going to do?' I asked: 'not surely to light a fire this hot evening? I shall be smothered.'

"'Indeed, Monsieur, I feel it very chilly since the rain began; besides, I must boil the water for my tea, for I take tea on Sundays; you will be obliged to bear the heat.'"

And Frances makes the tea, and sets the table, and brings out her pistolets, and offers them to Monsieur, and it is all very simple and idyllic. So is the scene where Crimsworth, without our knowing exactly how he does it, declares himself to Frances. The dialogue is half in French, and does not lend itself to quotation, but it compares very favourably with the more daring comedy of courtship in *Jane Eyre*. Frances is delicious in her very solidity, her absence of abandonment. She refuses flatly to give up her teaching at Crimsworth's desire, Crimsworth, who will have six thousand francs a year.

"'How rich you are, Monsieur!' And then she stirred uneasily in my arms. 'Three thousand francs!' she murmured, 'while I get only twelve hundred!' She went on faster. 'However, it must be so for the present; and, Monsieur, were you not saying something about my giving up my place? Oh no! I shall hold it fast'; and her little fingers emphatically tightened on mine.

"'Think of marrying you to be kept by you, Monsieur! I could not do it; and how dull my days would be! You would be away teaching in close, noisy schoolrooms, from morning till evening, and I should be lingering at home, unemployed and solitary. I should get depressed and sullen, and you would soon tire of me.'

"'Frances, you could yet read and study—two things you like so well.'

"'Monsieur, I could not; I like contemplative life, but I like an active better; I must act in some way, and act with you. I have taken notice, Monsieur, that people who are only in each other's company for amusement, never really like each other so well, or esteem each other so highly, as those who work together, and perhaps suffer together!'"

To which Crimsworth replies, "You speak God's truth, and you shall have your own way, for it is the best way."

There is far more common sense than passion in the solid little Frances and her apathetic lover. It is Frances Henri's situation, not her character, that recalls so irresistibly Lucy Snowe. Frances has neither Lucy's temperament, nor Lucy's terrible capacity for suffering. She suffers through her circumstances, not through her temperament. The motives handled in *The Professor* belong to the outer rather than the inner world; the pressure of circumstance, bereavement, poverty, the influences of alien and unloved surroundings, these are the springs that determine the drama of Frances and of Crimsworth. Charlotte is displaying a deliberate interest in the outer world and the material event.

She does not yet know that it is in the inner world that her great conquest and dominion is to be. The people in this first novel are of the same family as the people in *Jane Eyre*, in *Shirley*, in *Villette*. Crimsworth is almost reproduced in Louis Moore. Yorke Hunsden is the unmistakable father of Mr. Yorke and Rochester; Frances, a pale and passionless sister of Jane Eyre, and a first cousin of Lucy. Yet, in spite of these relationships, *The Professor* stands alone. In spite of its striking resemblance to *Villette* there is no real, no spiritual affinity. And the great gulf remains fixed between *The Professor* and *Jane Eyre*.

This difference lies deeper than technique. It is a difference of vision, of sensation. The strange greyness of *The Professor*, its stillness, is not due altogether to Charlotte's deliberate intention. It is the stillness, the greyness of imperfect hearing, of imperfect seeing. I know it has one fine piece of word-painting, but not one that can stand among Charlotte Brontë's masterpieces in this kind.

Here it is. "Already the pavement was drying; a balmy and fresh breeze stirred the air, purified by lightning; I left the west behind me, where spread a sky like opal, azure inmingled with crimson; the enlarged sun, glorious in Tyrian dyes, dipped his brim already; stepping, as I was, eastward, I faced a vast bank of clouds, but also I had before me the arch of an even rainbow; a perfect rainbow—high, wide, vivid. I looked long; my eye drank in the scene, and I suppose my brain must have absorbed it; for that night, after lying awake in pleasant fever a long time, watching the silent sheet-lightning, which still played among the retreating clouds, and flashed silvery over the stars, I at last fell asleep; and then in a dream was reproduced the setting sun, the bank of clouds, the mighty rainbow. I stood, methought, on a terrace; I leaned over a parapeted wall; there was space below me, depth I could not fathom, but hearing an endless splash of waves, I believed it to be the sea; sea spread to the horizon; sea of changeful green and intense blue; all was soft in the distance; all vapour-veiled. A spark of gold glistened on the line between water and air, floated up, appeared, enlarged, changed; the object hung midway between heaven and earth, under the arch of the rainbow; the soft but dark clouds diffused behind. It hovered as on wings; pearly, fleecy, gleaming air streamed like raiment round it; light, tinted with carnation, coloured what seemed face and limbs; a large star shone with still lustre on an angel's forehead—" But the angel ruins it.

And this is all, and it leaves the dreariness more dreary. In *The Professor* you wander through a world where there is no sound, no colour, no vibration; a world muffled and veiled in the stillness and the greyness of the hour before dawn. It is the work of a woman who is not perfectly alive. So far from having had her great awakening, Charlotte is only half awake. Her intellect is alert enough and avid, faithful and subservient to the fact. It is her nerves and senses that are asleep. Her soul is absent from her senses.

* * * * *

But in *Jane Eyre*, she is not only awakened, but awake as she has never been awake before, with all her virgin senses exquisitely alive, every nerve changed to intense vibration. Sometimes she is perniciously awake; she is doing appalling things, things unjustifiable, preposterous; things that would have meant perdition to any other writer; she sees with wild, erroneous eyes; but the point is that she sees, that she keeps moving, that from the first page to the last she is never once asleep. To come to *Jane Eyre* after *The Professor* is to pass into another world of feeling and of vision.

It is not the difference between reality and unreality. *The Professor* is real enough, more real in some minor points—dialogue, for instance—than *Jane Eyre*. The difference is that *The Professor* is a transcript of reality, a very delicate and faithful transcript, and *Jane Eyre* is reality itself, pressed on the senses. The pressure is so direct and so tremendous, that it lasts through those moments when the writer's grip has failed.

For there are moments, long moments of perfectly awful failure in *Jane Eyre*. There are phrases that make you writhe, such as "the etymology of the mansion's designation", and the shocking persistency with which Charlotte Brontë "indites", "peruses", and "retains". There are whole scenes that outrage probability. Such are the scenes, or parts of scenes, between Jane and Rochester during the comedy of his courtship. The great orchard scene does not ring entirely true. For pages and pages it falters between passion and melodrama; between rhetoric and the *cri de coeur*. Jane in the very thick of her emotion can say, "I have talked, face to face, with what I reverence, with what I delight in—with an original, a vigorous, an expanded mind. I have known you, Mr. Rochester, and it strikes me with terror and anguish to feel I absolutely must be torn from you for ever. I see the necessity for departure; and it is like looking on the necessity of death." And the comedy is worse. Jane elaborates too much in those delicious things she says to Rochester. Rochester himself provokes the parodist. (Such manners as Rochester's were unknown in mid-Victorian literature.)

"He continued to send for me punctually the moment the clock struck seven; though when I appeared before him now, he had no such honeyed terms as 'love' and 'darling' on his lips: the best words at my disposal were 'provoking', 'malicious elf', 'sprite', 'changeling', etc. For caresses, too, I now got grimaces; for a pressure of the hand, a pinch on the arm; for a kiss on the cheek, a severe tweak of the ear. It was all right: at present I decidedly preferred these fierce favours to anything more tender."

Yet there is comedy, pure comedy in those scenes, though never sustained, and never wrought to the inevitable dramatic climax. Jane is delightful when she asks Rochester whether the frown on his forehead will be his "married look", and when she tells him to make a dressing-gown for himself out of the pearl-grey silk, "and an infinite series of waistcoats out of the black satin". *The Quarterly* was much too hard on the earlier *cadeau* scene, with Rochester and Jane and Adèle, which is admirable in its suggestion of Jane's shyness and precision.

"'*N'est-ce pas, Monsieur, qu'il y a un cadeau pour Mademoiselle Eyre, dans votre petit coffre?*'"

"'Who talks of *cadeaux*?' said he gruffly; 'did you expect a present, Miss Eyre? Are you fond of presents?' and he searched my face with eyes that I saw were dark, irate, and piercing.

"'I hardly know, sir; I have little experience of them; they are generally thought pleasant things.'"

Charlotte Brontë was on her own ground there. But you tremble when she leaves it; you shudder throughout the awful drawing-room comedy of Blanche Ingram. Blanche says to her mother: "Am I right, Baroness Ingram of Ingram Park?" And her mother says to Blanche, "My lily-flower, you are right now, as always." Blanche says to Rochester, "Signor Eduardo, are you in voice to-night?" and he, "Donna Bianca, if you command it, I will be." And Blanche says to the footman, "Cease that chatter, blockhead, and do my bidding."

That, Charlotte's worst lapse, is a very brief one, and the scene itself is unimportant. But what can be said of the crucial scene of the novel, the tremendous scene of passion and temptation? There *is* passion in the scene before it, between Jane and Rochester on the afternoon of the wedding-day that brought no wedding.

"'Jane, I never meant to wound you thus. If the man who had but one little ewe lamb that was dear to him as a daughter, that ate of his bread, and drank of his cup, and lay in his bosom, had by some mistake slaughtered it at the shambles, he would not have rued his bloody blunder more than I now rue mine. Will you ever forgive me?'... 'You know I am a scoundrel, Jane?' ere long he inquired wistfully, wondering, I suppose, at my continued silence and tameness; the result of weakness rather than of will.

"'Yes, sir.'

"'Then tell me so roundly and sharply—don't spare me.'

"'I cannot; I am tired and sick. I want some water.'

"He heaved a sort of shuddering sigh, and, taking me in his

arms, carried me downstairs."

But there are terrible lapses. After Rochester's cry, "'Jane, my little darling ... If you were mad, do you think I should hate you,'" he elaborates his idea and he is impossible: "'Your mind is my treasure, and if it were broken it would be my treasure still; if you raved, my arms should confine you and not a strait waistcoat—your grasp, even in fury, would have a charm for me; if you flew at me as wildly as that woman did this morning, I should receive you in an embrace at least as fond as it would be restrictive.'"

And in the final scene of temptation there is a most curious mingling of reality and unreality, of the passion which is poetry, and the poetry which is not passion.

"'Never,' said he, as he ground his teeth, 'never was anything so frail, and so indomitable. A mere reed she feels in my hand!' And he shook me with the force of his hold. 'I could bend her with my finger and thumb; and what good would it do if I bent, if I uptore, if I crushed her? Consider that eye: consider the resolute, wild, free thing looking out of it, defying me, with more than courage—with a stern triumph. Whatever I do with its cage, I cannot get at it—the savage, beautiful creature! If I tear, if I rend the slight prison, my outrage will only let the captive loose. Conqueror I might be of the house; but the inmate would escape to heaven before I could call myself possessor of its clay dwelling-place. And it is you, spirit—with will and energy, and virtue and purity—that I want: not alone your brittle frame. Of yourself, you could come with soft flight and nestle against my heart, if you would; seized against your will you will elude the grasp like an essence—you will vanish ere I inhale your fragrance. Oh, come, Jane, come!'"

It is the crucial scene of the book; and with all its power, with all its vehemence and passionate reality it is unconvincing. It stirs you and it leaves you cold.

The truth is that in *Jane Eyre* Charlotte Brontë had not mastered the art of dialogue; and to the very last she was uncertain in her handling of it. In this she is inferior to all the great novelists of her time; inferior to some who were by no means great. She understood more of the spiritual speech of passion than any woman before her, but she ignores its actual expression, its violences, its reticences, its silences. In her great scenes she is inspired one moment, and the next positively handicapped by her passion and her poetry. In the same sentence she rises to the sudden poignant *cri du coeur*, and sinks to the artifice of metaphor. She knew that passion is poetry, and poetry is passion; you might say it was all she knew, or ever cared to know. But her language of passion is too often the language of written rather than of spoken poetry, of poetry that is not poetry at all. It is as if she had never heard the speech of living men and women. There is more actuality in the half-French chatter of Adèle than in any of the high utterances of Jane and Rochester.

And yet her sense of the emotion behind the utterance is infallible, so infallible that we accept the utterance. By some miracle, which is her secret, the passion gets through. The illusion of reality is so strong that it covers its own lapses. *Jane Eyre* exists to prove that truth is higher than actuality.

"'Jane suits me: do I suit her?'"

"'To the finest fibre of my nature, sir.'"

If no woman alive had ever said that, it would yet be true to Jane's feeling. For it is a matter of the finest fibres, this passion of Jane's, that set people wondering about Currer Bell, that inflamed Mrs. Oliphant, as it inflamed the reviewer in *The Quarterly*, and made Charles Kingsley think that Currer Bell was coarse. Their state of mind is incredible to us now. For what did poor Jane do, after all? Nobody could possibly have had more respect for the ten commandments. For all Rochester's raging, the ten commandments remain exactly where they were. It was inconceivable to Charlotte Brontë that any decent man or woman could make hay, or wish to make hay, of them. And yet Jane offended. She sinned against the unwritten code that ordains that a woman may lie till she is purple in the face, but she must not, as a piece of gratuitous information, tell a man she loves him; not, that is to say, in as many words. She may declare her passion unmistakably in other ways. She may exhibit every ignominious and sickly sign of it; her eyes may glow like hot coals; she may tremble; she may flush and turn pale; she may do almost anything, provided she does not speak the actual words. In mid-Victorian times an enormous licence was allowed her. She might faint, with perfect propriety, in public; she might become anaemic and send for the doctor, and be ordered iron; she might fall ill, horridly and visibly, and have to be taken away to spas and places to drink the waters. Everybody knew what that meant. If she had shrieked her passion on the housetops she could hardly have published it more violently; but nobody minded. It was part of the mid-Victorian convention.

Jane Eyre did none of these things. As soon as she was aware of her passion for Mr. Rochester she thrust it down into the pocket of her voluminous mid-Victorian skirt and sat on it. Instead of languishing and fainting where Rochester could see her, she held her head rather higher than usual, and practised the spirited arts of retort and repartee. And nobody gave her any credit for it. Then Rochester puts the little thing (poor Jane was only eighteen when it happened) to the torture, and, with the last excruciating turn of the thumbscrew, she confesses. That was the enormity that was never forgiven her.

"'You'll like Ireland, I think,'" says Rochester in his torturing mood; "'they are such kind-hearted people there.'

"'It is a long way off, sir.'

"'No matter, a girl of your sense will not object to the voyage or the distance.'

"'Not the voyage, but the distance: and then the sea is a barrier.'

"'From what, Jane?'

"'From England and from Thornfield, and—'

"'Well?'

"'From *you*, sir.'"

She had done it. She had said, or almost said the words.

It just happened. There was magic in the orchard at Thornfield;

there was youth in her blood; and—"Jane, did you hear the nightingale singing in that wood?"

Still, she had done it.

And she was the first heroine who had. Adultery, with which we are fairly familiar, would have seemed a lesser sin. There may be extenuating circumstances for the adulteress. There were extenuating circumstances for Rochester. He could plead a wife who went on all fours. There were no extenuating circumstances for little Jane. No use for her to say that she was upset by the singing of the nightingale; that it didn't matter what she said to Mr. Rochester when Mr. Rochester was going to marry Blanche Ingram, anyway; that she only flung herself at his head because she knew she couldn't hit it; that her plainness gave her a certain licence, placing her beyond the code. Not a bit of it. Jane's plainness was one thing that they had against her. Until her time no heroine had been permitted to be plain. Jane's seizing of the position was part of the general insolence of her behaviour.

Jane's insolence was indeed unparalleled. Having done the deed she felt no shame or sense of sin; she stood straight up and defended herself. That showed that she was hardened.

It certainly showed—Jane's refusal to be abject—that Jane was far ahead of her age.

"'I tell you I must go!' I retorted, roused to something like passion. 'Do you think I can stay to become nothing to you? Do you think I am an automaton?—a machine without feelings, and can bear to have my morsel of bread snatched from my lips, and my drop of living water dashed from my cup? Do you think, because I am poor, obscure, plain and little, I am soulless and heartless? You think wrong! I have as much soul as you, and fully as much heart! And if God had gifted me with some beauty and much wealth, I should have made it as hard for you to leave me as it is now for me to leave you. I am not talking to you now through the medium of custom, conventionalities, or even of mortal flesh: it is my spirit that addresses'" ("Addresses"? oh, Jane!) "'your spirit; just as if both had passed through the grave, and we stood at God's feet, equal—as we are!'"

This, allowing for some slight difference in the phrasing, is twentieth century. And it was this—Jane's behaviour in the orchard, and not Rochester's behaviour in the past—that opened the door to the "imps of evil meaning, polluting and defiling the domestic hearth."

Still, though *The Quarterly* censured Jane's behaviour, it was Rochester who caused most of the trouble and the scandal by his remarkable confessions. In a sense they *were* remarkable. Seldom, outside the pages of French fiction, had there been so lavish and public a display of mistresses. And while it was agreed on all hands that Rochester was incredible with his easy references to Céline and Giacinta and Clara, still more incredible was it that a young woman in a country parsonage should have realized so much as the existence of Clara and Giacinta and Céline. But, when Mrs. Gaskell and Madame Duclaux invoked Branwell and all his vices to account for Charlotte's experience, they forgot that Charlotte had read Balzac,[A] and that Balzac is an experience in himself. She had also read Moore's *Life of Byron*, and really there is nothing in Rochester's confessions that Byron and a little Balzac would not account for. So that they might just as well have left poor Branwell in his grave.

> [Footnote A: I am wrong. Charlotte did not read Balzac till later, when George Henry Lewes told her to. But there were those twenty "clever, wicked, sophistical, and immoral French books" that she read in eighteen-forty. They may have served her purpose better.]

Indeed, it was the manner of Rochester's confession that gave away the secret of Currer Bell's sex; her handling of it is so inadequate and perfunctory. Rochester is at his worst and most improbable in the telling of his tale. The tale in itself is one of Charlotte's clumsiest contrivances for conveying necessary information. The alternate baldness and exuberant, decorated, swaggering boldness (for Charlotte's style was never bolder than when she was essaying the impossible) alone betrayed the hand of an innocent woman. Curious that these makeshift passages with their obviously second-hand material, their palpably alien *mise en scène*, should ever have suggested a personal experience and provoked *The Quarterly* to its infamous and immortal utterance: "If we ascribe the book to a woman at all, we have no alternative but to ascribe it to one who has, for some sufficient reason, long forfeited the society of her own sex."

The Quarterly, to do it justice, argued that Currer Bell was a man, for only a man would have betrayed such ignorance of feminine resources as to make Jane Eyre, on a night alarm, "hurry on a frock and shawl". The reasoning passed. Nobody saw that such a man would be as innocent as any parson's daughter. Nobody pointed out that, as it happened, Currer Bell had provided her dowagers with "vast white wrappers" on the second night alarm. And, after all, the sex of *The Quarterly* reviewer itself remains a problem. Long ago Mr. Andrew Lang detected the work of two hands in that famous article. You may say there were at least three. There was, first, the genial reviewer of *Vanity Fair*, who revels in the wickedness of Becky Sharpe, and who is going to revel in the wickedness of Jane. Then suddenly some Mr. Brocklebank steps in, and you get a "black-marble clergyman" on *Jane Eyre*.

"We have said," says this person, "that this was the picture of a natural heart. This, to our view, is the great and crying mischief of the book. Jane Eyre is throughout the personification of an unregenerate and undisciplined spirit, the more dangerous to exhibit from that prestige of principle and self-control, which is liable to dazzle the eyes too much for it to observe the insufficient and unsound foundation on which it rests. It is true Jane does right, and exerts great moral strength; but it is the strength of a mere heathen mind which is a law unto itself.... She has inherited the worst sin of our fallen nature—the sin of pride."

Jane, you see, should have sinned to show her Christian

humility. The style, if not the reasoning, is pure Brocklebank. He does "not hesitate to say that the tone of mind and thought, which has overthrown authority and violated every code, human and divine, abroad, and fostered Chartism and rebellion at home, is the same which has written *Jane Eyre*".

Ellis and Acton (poor Acton!) Bell get it even stronger than that; and then, suddenly again, you come on a report on the "Condition of Governesses", palpably drawn up by a third person. For years Miss Rigby, who was afterwards Lady Eastlake, got the credit for the whole absurd performance, for she was known to have written the review on *Vanity Fair*. What happened seems to have been that Miss Rigby set out in all honesty to praise *Jane Eyre*. Then some infuriated person interfered and stopped her. The article was torn from the unfortunate Miss Rigby and given to Brocklebank, who used bits of her here and there. Brocklebank, in his zeal, overdid his part, so the report on Governesses was thrown in to give the whole thing an air of seriousness and respectability. So that it is exceedingly doubtful whether, after all, it was a woman's hand that dealt the blow.

If Charlotte Brontë did not feel the effect of it to the end of her life, she certainly suffered severely at the time. It was responsible for that impassioned defence of Anne and Emily which she would have been wiser to have left alone.

It must be admitted that *Jane Eyre* was an easy prey for the truculent reviewer, for its faults were all on the surface, and its great qualities lay deep. Deep as they were, they gripped the ordinary uncritical reader, and they gripped the critic in spite of himself, so that he bitterly resented being moved by a work so flagrantly and obviously faulty. What was more, the passion of the book was so intense that you were hardly aware of anything else, and its author's austere respect for the ten commandments passed almost unobserved.

But when her enemies accuse Charlotte Brontë of glorifying passion they praise her unaware. Her glory is that she did glorify it. Until she came, passion between man and woman had meant animal passion. Fielding and Smollett had dealt with it solely on that footing. A woman's gentle, legalized affection for her husband was one thing, and passion was another. Thackeray and Dickens, on the whole, followed Fielding. To all three of them passion is an affair wholly of the senses, temporary, episodic, and therefore comparatively unimportant. Thackeray intimated that he could have done more with it but for his fear of Mrs. Grundy. Anyhow, passion was not a quality that could be given to a good woman; and so the good women of Dickens and Thackeray are conspicuously without it. And Jane Austen may be said to have also taken Fielding's view. Therefore she was obliged to ignore passion. She gave it to one vulgar woman, Lydia Bennett, and to one bad one, Mrs. Rushworth; and having given it them, she turned her head away and refused to have anything more to do with these young women. She was not alone in her inability to "tackle passion". No respectable mid-Victorian novelist could, when passion had so bad a name.

And it was this thing, cast down, defiled, dragged in the mud, and ignored because of its defilement, that Charlotte Brontë took and lifted up. She washed it clean; she bathed it in the dew of the morning; she baptized it in tears; she clothed it in light and flame; she showed it for the divine, the beautiful, the utterly pure and radiant thing it is, "the very sublime of faith, truth and devotion". She made it, this spirit of fire and air, incarnate in the body of a woman who had no sensual charm. Because of it little Jane became the parent of Caterina and of Maggie Tulliver; and Shirley prepared the way for Meredith's large-limbed, large-brained, large-hearted women.

It was thus that Charlotte Brontë glorified passion. The passion that she glorified being of the finest fibre, it was naturally not understood by people whose fibres were not fine at all.

It was George Henry Lewes (not a person of the finest fibre) who said of *Jane Eyre* that "the grand secret of its success ... as of all great and lasting successes was its reality". In spite of crudities, absurdities, impossibilities, it remains most singularly and startlingly alive. In *Jane Eyre* Charlotte Brontë comes for the first time into her kingdom of the inner life. She grasps the secret, unseen springs; in her narrow range she is master of the psychology of passion and of suffering, whether she is describing the agony of the child Jane shut up in that terrible red room, or the anguish of the woman on the morning of that wedding-day that brought no wedding. Or take the scene of Jane's flight from Thornfield, or that other scene, unsurpassed in its passion and tenderness, of her return to Rochester at Ferndean.

"To this house I came just ere dark, on an evening marked by the characteristics of sad sky, cold gale, and continued small, penetrating rain.... Even within a very short distance of the manor-house you could see nothing of it; so thick and dark grew the timber of the gloomy wood about it. Iron gates between granite pillars showed me where to enter, and passing through them, I found myself at once in the twilight of close-ranked trees. There was a grass-grown track descending the forest aisle, between hoar and knotty shafts and under branched arches. I followed it, expecting soon to reach the dwelling; but it stretched on and on, it wound far and farther: no sign of habitation or grounds was visible.... At last my way opened, the trees thinned a little; presently I beheld a railing, then the house—scarce, by this dim light, distinguishable from the trees; so dank and green were its decaying walls. Entering a portal, fastened only by a latch, I stood amidst a space of enclosed ground, from which the wood swept away in a semicircle. There were no flowers, no garden-beds; only a broad gravel-walk girdling a grass-plat, and this set in the heavy frame of the forest. The house presented two pointed gables in its front; the windows were latticed and narrow: the front-door was narrow too, one step led up to it.... It was still as a church on a week-day; the pattering rain on the forest leaves was the only sound audible....

"I heard a movement—that narrow front-door was unclosing, and some shape was about to issue from the grange.

"It opened slowly; a figure came out into the twilight and stood on the step; a man without a hat: he stretched forth his hand as if to feel whether it rained. Dark as it was I had recognized him....

"His form was of the same strong and stalwart contour as ever.... But in his countenance I saw a change: that looked desperate and brooding—that reminded me of some wronged and fettered wild beast or bird, dangerous to approach in his sullen woe. The caged eagle, whose gold-ringed eyes cruelty has extinguished, might look as looked that sightless Samson."

Again—Rochester hears Jane's voice in the room where she comes to him.

"'And where is the speaker? Is it only a voice? Oh! I *cannot* see, but I must feel or my heart will stop and my brain burst.'...

"He groped. I arrested his wandering hand, and prisoned it in both mine.

"'Her very fingers!' he cried; 'her small, slight fingers! If so, there must be more of her.'

"The muscular hand broke from my custody; my arm was seized, my shoulder—neck—wrist—I was entwined and gathered to him....

"I pressed my lips to his once brilliant and now rayless eyes—I swept back his hair from his brow and kissed that too. He suddenly seemed to rouse himself: the conviction of the reality of all this seized him.

"'It is you—is it, Jane? You are come back to me then?'

"'I am.'"

The scene as it stands is far from perfect; but only Charlotte Brontë could sustain so strong an illusion of passion through so many lapses. And all that passion counts for no more than half in the astounding effect of reality she produces. Before *Jane Eyre* there is no novel written by a woman, with the one exception of *Wuthering Heights*, that conveys so poignant an impression of surroundings, of things seen and heard, of the earth and sky; of weather; of the aspects of houses and of rooms. It suggests a positive exaltation of the senses of sound and light, an ecstasy, an enchantment before the visible, tangible world. It is not a matter of mere faithful observation (though few painters have possessed so incorruptibly the innocence of the eye). It is an almost supernatural intentness; sensation raised to the nth power. Take the description of the awful red room at Gateshead.

"A bed supported on massive pillars of mahogany, hung with curtains of deep red damask, stood out like a tabernacle in the centre; the two large windows with their blinds always drawn down, were half shrouded in festoons and falls of similar drapery; the carpet was red; the table at the foot of the bed was covered with a crimson cloth; the walls were a soft fawn colour, with a flush of pink in it; the wardrobe, the toilet-table, the chairs were of darkly-polished old mahogany. Out of these deep surrounding shades rose high and glared white the piled-up mattresses and pillows of the bed, spread with a snowy Marseilles counterpane. Scarcely less prominent was an ample, cushioned easy-chair near the head of the bed, also white, with a footstool before it; and looking, as I thought, like a pale throne.... Mr. Reed had been dead nine years: it was in this chamber he breathed his last; here he lay in state; hence his coffin was borne by the undertaker's men; and since that day a sense of dreary consecration had guarded it from frequent intrusion."

Could anything be more horrible than that red room? Or take the descriptions of the school at Lowood where the horror of pestilence hangs over house and garden. Through all these Gateshead and Lowood scenes Charlotte is unerring and absolute in her reality.

Her very style, so uncertain in its rendering of human speech, becomes flawless in such passages as this: "It was three o'clock; the church-bell tolled as I passed under the belfry: the charm of the hour lay in its approaching dimness, in the low-gliding and pale-beaming sun. I was a mile from Thornfield, in a lane noted for wild roses in summer, for nuts and blackberries in autumn, and even now possessing a few coral treasures in hips and haws, but whose best winter delight lay in its utter solitude and leafless repose. If a breath of air stirred, it made no sound here; for there was not a holly, not an evergreen to rustle, and the stripped hawthorn and hazel bushes were as still as the white, worn stones which causewayed the middle of the path. Far and wide, on each side, there were only fields, where no cattle now browsed; and the little brown birds, which stirred occasionally in the hedge, looked like single russet leaves about to drop.

"This lane inclined up-hill all the way to Hay.... I then turned eastward.

"On the hill-top above me sat the rising moon; pale yet as a cloud, but brightening momently; she looked over Hay which, half lost in trees, sent up a blue smoke from its few chimneys; it was yet a mile distant, but in the absolute hush I could hear plainly its thin murmurs of life. My ear, too, felt the flow of currents; in what dales and depths I could not tell: but there were many hills beyond Hay, and doubtless many becks threading their passes. That evening calm betrayed alike the tinkle of the nearest streams, the sough of the most remote.

"A rude noise broke on these fine ripplings and whisperings, at once so far away and so clear: a positive tramp, tramp; a metallic clatter, which effaced the soft wave-wanderings; as, in a picture, the solid mass of a crag, or the rough boles of a great oak, drawn in dark and strong on the foreground, efface the aerial distance of azure hill, sunny horizon, and blended clouds, where tint melts into tint.

"The din sounded on the causeway...."

Flawless this, too, of the sky after sunset: "Where the sun had gone down in simple state—pure of the pomp of clouds—spread a solemn purple, burning with the light of red jewel and furnace flame at one point, on one hill-peak, and extending high and wide, soft and still softer, over half heaven."

And this of her own moors: "There are great moors behind and on each hand of me; there are waves of mountains far beyond that deep valley at my feet. The population here must be thin, and I see no passengers on these roads: they stretch out east, west, north and south—white, broad, lonely; they are all cut in the moor, and the heather grows deep and wild to their very verge."

She has given the secret of the moor country in a phrase: "I felt the consecration of its loneliness." In that one line you have the real, the undying Charlotte Brontë.

It is such immortal things that make the difference between *Jane Eyre* and *The Professor*. So immeasurable is that difference that it almost justifies the theorist in assuming an "experience" to account for it, an experience falling between the dates of *The Professor* and *Jane Eyre*. Unfortunately there was none; none in the sense cherished by the researcher. Charlotte's letters are an unbroken record of those two years that followed her return from Brussels. Her life is laid bare in its long and cramped monotony, a life singularly empty of "experience".

And yet an experience did come to her in that brief period. If the researcher had not followed a false scent across the Channel, if his *flair* for tragic passion had not destroyed in him all sense of proportion, he could not possibly have missed it; for it stared him in the face, simple, obvious, inevitable. But miss it he certainly did. Obsessed by his idea, he considered it a negligible circumstance that Charlotte should have read *Wuthering Heights* before she wrote *Jane Eyre*. And yet, I think that, if anything woke Charlotte up, it was that. Until then, however great her certainty of her own genius, she did not know how far she could trust it, how far it would be safe to let imagination go. Appalled by the spectacle of its excesses, she had divorced imagination from the real. But Emily knew none of these cold deliberations born of fear. *Wuthering Heights* was the fruit of a divine freedom, a divine unconsciousness. It is not possible that Charlotte, of all people, should have read *Wuthering Heights* without a shock of enlightenment; that she should not have compared it with her own bloodless work; that she should not have felt the wrong done to her genius by her self-repression. Emily had dared to be herself; *she* had not been afraid of her own passion; she had had no method; she had accomplished a stupendous thing without knowing it, by simply letting herself go. And Charlotte, I think, said to herself, "That is what I ought to have done. That is what I will do next time." And next time she did it. The experience may seem insufficient, but it is of such experiences that a great writer's life is largely made. And if you *must* have an influence to account for *Jane Eyre*, there is no need to go abroad to look for it. There was influence enough in her own home. These three Brontës, adoring each other, were intolerant of any other influence; and the strongest spirit, which was Emily's, prevailed. To be sure, no remonstrances from Emily or Charlotte could stop Anne in her obstinate analysis of Walter Huntingdon; but it was some stray spark from Emily that kindled Anne. As for Charlotte, her genius must have quickened in her when her nerves thrilled to the shock of *Wuthering Heights*. This, I know, is only another theory; but it has at least the merit of its modesty. It is not offered as in the least accounting for, or explaining, Charlotte's genius. It merely suggests with all possible humility a likely cause of its release. Anyhow, it is a theory that does Charlotte's genius no wrong, on which account it seems to me preferable to any other. It is really no argument against it to say that Charlotte never acknowledged her sister's influence, that she was indeed unaware of it; for, in the first place, the stronger the spiritual tie between them, the less likely was she to have been aware. In the second place, it is not claimed that *Wuthering Heights* was such an influence as the "sojourn in Brussels" is said to have been—that it "made Miss Brontë an author". It is not claimed that if there had been no *Wuthering Heights* and no Emily Brontë, there would have been no *Jane Eyre*; for to me nothing can be more certain that whatever had, or had not happened, Charlotte's genius would have found its way.

Charlotte's genius indeed was so profoundly akin to Charlotte's nature that its way, the way of its upward progress, was by violent impetus and recoil.

In *Shirley* she revolts from the passion of *Jane Eyre*. She seems to have written it to prove that there are other things. She had been stung by *The Quarterly's* attack, stung by rumour, stung by every adverse thing that had been said. And yet not for a moment was she "influenced" by her reviewers. It was more in defiance than in submission that she answered them with *Shirley*. *Shirley* was an answer to every criticism that had yet been made. In *Shirley* she forsook the one poor play of hearts insurgent for the vast and varied movement of the world; social upheavals, the clash of sects and castes, the first grim hand-to-hand struggle between capital and labour, all are there. The book opens with a drama, not of hearts but of artisans insurgent; frame-breakers, not breakers of the marriage law. In sheer defiance she essays to render the whole real world, the complex, many-threaded, many-coloured world; where the tragic warp is woven with the bright comedy of curates. It is the world of the beginnings; the world of the early nineteenth century that she paints. A world with the immensity, the profundity, the darkness of the brooding sea; where the spirit of a woman moves, troubling the waters; for Charlotte Brontë has before her the stupendous vision of the world as it was, as it yet is, and as it is to be.

That world, as it existed from eighteen-twelve to Charlotte's own time, eighteen-fifty, was not a place for a woman with a brain and a soul. There was no career for any woman but marriage. If she missed it she missed her place in the world, her prestige, and her privileges as a woman. What was worse, she lost her individuality, and became a mere piece of furniture, of disused, old-fashioned furniture, in her father's or her brother's house. If she had a father or a brother there was no escape for her from dependence on the male; and if she had none, if there was no male about the house, her case was the more pitiable. And the traditions of her upbringing were such that the real, vital things, the things that mattered, were never mentioned in her presence. Religion was the solitary exception; and religion had the reality and vitality taken out of it by its dissociation with the rest of life. A woman in these horrible conditions was only half alive. She had no energies, no passions, no enthusiasms. Convention drained her of her life-blood. What was left to her had no outlet; pent up in her, it bred weak, anaemic substitutes for its natural issue, sentimentalism for passion, and sensibility for the nerves of vision. This only applies, of course, to the average woman.

Charlotte Brontë was born with a horror of the world that had produced this average woman, this creature of minute corruptions and hypocrisies. She sent out *Jane Eyre* to purify it with her passion. She sent out *Shirley* to destroy and rebuild it with her intellect. Little Jane was a fiery portent. Shirley was a prophecy. She is modern to her finger-tips, as modern as Meredith's great women: Diana, or Clara Middleton, or Carinthia Jane. She was born fifty years before her time.

This is partly owing to her creator's prophetic insight, partly to her sheer truth to life. For Shirley was to a large extent a portrait of Emily Brontë who was born before her time.

It is Emily Brontë's spirit that burns in Shirley Keeldar; and it is the spirit of Shirley Keeldar that gives life to the unwilling mass of this vast novel. It is almost enough immortality for Shirley that she is the only living and authentic portrait of Emily Brontë in her time. Charlotte has given her the "wings that wealth can give", and they do not matter. She has also given her the wings of Emily's adventurous soul, the wealth of her inner life.

"A still, deep, inborn delight glows in her young veins; unmingled—untroubled, not to be reached or ravished by human agency, because by no human agency bestowed: the pure gift of God to His creature, the free dower of Nature to her child. This joy gives her experience of a genii-life. Buoyant, by green steps, by glad hills, all verdure and light, she reaches a station scarcely lower than that whence angels looked down on the dreamer of Bethel, and her eye seeks, and her soul possesses, the vision of life as she wishes it."

"Her eye seeks, and her soul possesses, the vision of life as she wishes it—" That was the secret of Emily's greatness, of her immeasurable superiority to her sad sisters.

And again: "In Shirley's nature prevailed at times an easy

indolence: there were periods when she took delight in perfect vacancy of hand and eye—moments when her thoughts, her simple existence, the fact of the world being around—and heaven above her, seemed to yield her such fulness of happiness, that she did not need to lift a finger to increase the joy. Often, after an active morning, she would spend a sunny afternoon in lying stirless on the turf, at the foot of some tree of friendly umbrage: no society did she need but that of Caroline, and it sufficed if she were within call; no spectacle did she ask but that of the deep blue sky, and such cloudlets as sailed afar and aloft across its span; no sound but that of the bee's hum, the leaf's whisper."

There are phrases in Louis Moore's diary that bring Emily Brontë straight before us in her swift and vivid life. Shirley is "Sister of the spotted, bright, quick-fiery leopard." "Pantheress!—beautiful forest-born!—wily, tameless, peerless nature! She gnaws her chain. I see the white teeth working at the steel! She has dreams of her wild woods, and pinings after virgin freedom." "How evanescent, fugitive, fitful she looked—slim and swift as a Northern streamer!" "... With her long hair flowing full and wavy; with her noiseless step, her pale cheek, her eye full of night and lightning, she looked, I thought, spirit-like—a thing made of an element—the child of a breeze and a flame—the daughter of ray and raindrop—a thing never to be overtaken, arrested, fixed."

Like Emily she is not "caught". "But if I were," she says, "do you know what soothsayers I would consult?... The little Irish beggar that comes barefoot to my door; the mouse that steals out of the cranny in the wainscot; the bird that in frost and snow pecks at my window for a crumb; the dog that licks my hand and sits beside my knee."

And yet again: "She takes her sewing occasionally: but, by some fatality, she is doomed never to sit steadily at it for above five minutes at a time: her thimble is scarcely fitted on, her needle scarce threaded, when a sudden thought calls her upstairs; perhaps she goes to seek some just-then-remembered old ivory-backed needle-book, or older china-topped work-box, quite unneeded, but which seems at the moment indispensable; perhaps to arrange her hair, or a drawer which she recollects to have seen that morning in a state of curious confusion; perhaps only to take a peep from a particular window at a particular view where Briarfield Church and Rectory are visible, pleasantly bowered in trees. She has scarcely returned, and again taken up the slip of cambric, or square of half-wrought canvas, when Tartar's bold scrape and strangled whistle are heard at the porch door, and she must run to open it for him; it is a hot day; he comes in panting; she must convoy him to the kitchen, and see with her own eyes that his water-bowl is replenished. Through the open kitchen-door the court is visible, all sunny and gay, and peopled with turkeys and their poults, peahens and their chicks, pearl-flecked Guinea fowls, and a bright variety of pure white and purple-necked, and blue and cinnamon-plumed pigeons. Irresistible spectacle to Shirley! She runs to the pantry for a roll, and she stands on the doorstep scattering crumbs: around her throng her eager, plump, happy, feathered vassals.... There are perhaps some little calves, some little new-yeaned lambs—it may be twins, whose mothers have rejected them: Miss Keeldar ... must permit herself the treat of feeding them with her own hand."

Like Emily she is impatient of rituals and creeds. Like Emily she adores the Earth. Not one of Charlotte's women except Shirley could have chanted that great prose hymn of adoration in which Earth worships and is worshipped. "'Nature is now at her evening prayers; she is kneeling before those red hills. I see her prostrate on the great steps of her altar, praying for a fair night for mariners at sea, for travellers in deserts, for lambs on moors, and unfledged birds in woods.... I see her, and I will tell you what she is like: she is like what Eve was when she and Adam stood alone on earth.' 'And that is not Milton's Eve, Shirley,' says Caroline, and Shirley answers: 'No, by the pure Mother of God, she is not.' Shirley is half a Pagan. She would beg to remind

Milton 'that the first men of the earth were Titans, and that Eve was their mother: from her sprang Saturn, Hyperion, Oceanus; she bore Prometheus…. I say, there were giants on the earth in those days, giants that strove to scale heaven. The first woman's breast that heaved with life on this world yielded daring which could contend with Omnipotence; the strength which could bear a thousand years of bondage—the vitality which could feed that vulture death through uncounted ages—the unexhausted life and uncorrupted excellence, sisters to immortality, which, after millenniums of crimes, struggles, and woes, could conceive and bring forth a Messiah. The first woman was heaven-born: vast was the heart whence gushed the well-spring of the blood of nations; and grand the undegenerate head where rested the consort-crown of creation.'…

"'You have not yet told me what you saw kneeling on those hills.'

"'I saw—I now see—a woman-Titan; her robe of blue air spreads to the outskirts of the heath, where yonder flock is grazing; a veil, white as an avalanche, sweeps from her head to her feet, and arabesques of lightning flame on its borders. Under her breast I see her zone, purple like that horizon: through its blush shines the star of evening. Her steady eyes I cannot picture; they are clear—they are deep as lakes—they are lifted and full of worship—they tremble with the softness of love and the lustre of prayer. Her forehead has the expanse of a cloud, and is paler than the early moon, risen long before dark gathers: she reclines her bosom on the edge of Stilbro' Moor; her mighty hands are joined beneath it. So kneeling, face to face, she speaks with God.'"

It is the living sister speaking for the dead; for Charlotte herself had little of Emily's fine Paganism. But for one moment, in this lyric passage, her soul echoes the very soul of Emily as she gathers round her all the powers and splendours (and some, alas, of the fatal rhetoric) of her prose to do her honour.

It is not only in the large figure of the Titan Shirley that Charlotte Brontë shows her strength. She has learnt to draw her minor masculine characters with more of insight and of accuracy—Caroline Helstone, the Yorkes, Robert Moore, Mr. Helstone, Joe Scott, and Barraclough, the "joined Methody". With a few strokes they stand out living. She has acquired more of the art of dialogue. She is a past master of dialect, of the racy, native speech of these men. Not only is Mr. Yorke painted with unerring power and faithfulness in every detail of his harsh and vigorous personality, but there is no single lapse from nature when he is speaking. The curates only excepted, Charlotte never swerves from this fidelity. But when she is handling her curates, it is a savage and utterly inartistic humour that inspires her. You feel that she is not exercising the art of comedy, but relieving her own intolerable boredom and irritation. No object could well be more innocent, and more appealing in its innocence, than little Mr. Sweeting, curate of Nunnerly. Mr. Sweeting at the tea-table, "having a dish of tarts before him, and marmalade and crumpet upon his plate", should have moved the Comic Spirit to tears of gentleness.

Curates apart, two-thirds of *Shirley* are written with an unerring devotion to the real, to the very actual. They have not, for all that, the profound reality of *Jane Eyre*. The events are confused, somehow; the atmosphere is confusing; the northern background is drawn with a certain hardness and apathy of touch; the large outlines are obscured, delicate colours sharpened; it is hard and yet blurred, like a bad steel engraving. Charlotte's senses, so intensely, so supernaturally alive in *Jane Eyre*, are only passably awake in *Shirley*. It has some of the dulness of *The Professor*, as it has more than its sober rightness. But, for three-and-twenty chapters, the sobriety, the rightness triumph. There are no improbabilities, no flights of imagination, none of the fine language which was the shame when it was not the glory of *Jane Eyre*.

Then suddenly there comes a break—a cleavage. It comes with that Chapter Twenty-four, which is headed "The Valley of the Shadow of Death". It was written in the first months after Emily Brontë's death.

From that point Charlotte's level strength deserts her. Ever after, she falls and soars, and soars and falls again. There is a return to the manner of *Jane Eyre*, the manner of Charlotte when she is deeply moved; there is at times a relapse to Jane Eyre's worst manner. You get it at once in "The Valley of the Shadow" chapter, in the scene of Caroline's love-sick delirium.

"'But he will not know I am ill till I am gone; and he will come when they have laid me out, and I am senseless, cold and stiff.

"'What can my departed soul feel then? Can it see or know what happens to the clay? Can spirits, through any medium, communicate with living flesh? Can the dead at all revisit those they leave? Can they come in the elements? Will wind, water, fire lend me a path to Moore?

"'Is it for nothing the wind sounds almost articulate sometimes—sings as I have lately heard it sing at night—or passes the casement sobbing, as if for sorrow to come? Does nothing then haunt it—nothing inspire it?'"

The awful improbability of Caroline is more striking because of its contrast with the inspired rightness of the scene of Cathy's delirium in *Wuthering Heights*. It is Charlotte feebly echoing Emily, and going more and more wrong up to her peroration.

Delirious Caroline wonders: "'What is that electricity they speak of, whose changes make us well or ill; whose lack or excess blasts; whose even balance revives?...'

"'*Where* is the other world? In *what* will another life consist? Why do I ask? Have I not cause to think that the hour is hasting but too fast when the veil must be rent for me? Do I not know the Grand Mystery is likely to break prematurely on me? Great Spirit, in whose goodness I confide; whom, as my Father, I have petitioned night and morning from early infancy, help the weak creation of Thy hands! Sustain me through the ordeal I dread and must undergo! Give me strength! Give me patience! Give me—oh, *give me* FAITH!'"

Jane Eyre has done worse than that, so has Rochester; but

somehow, when they were doing their worst with it, they got their passion through. There is no live passion behind this speech of Caroline's, with its wild stress of italics and of capitals. What passion there was in Charlotte when she conceived Caroline was killed by Emily's death.

And Mrs. Pryor, revealing herself to Caroline, is even more terrible. She has all the worst vices of Charlotte's dramatic style. Mrs. Pryor calls to the spirit of Caroline's dead father: "'James, slumber peacefully! See, your terrible debt is cancelled! Look! I wipe out the long, black account with my own hand! James, your child atones: this living likeness of you—this thing with your perfect features—this one good gift you gave me has nestled affectionately to my heart and tenderly called me "mother". Husband, rest forgiven.'"

Even Robert Moore, otherwise almost a masterpiece, becomes improbable when, in his great scene, Shirley refuses him. When Mr. Yorke asks him what has gone wrong he replies: "The machinery of all my nature; the whole enginery of this human mill; the boiler, which I take to be the heart, is fit to burst."

Shirley herself is impossible with her "Lucifer, Star of the Morning, thou art fallen," and her speech to her mercenary uncle: "Sir, your god, your great Bell, your fish-tailed Dagon, rises before me as a demon."

What is worse than all, Louis Moore—Louis, the hero, Louis, the master of passion, is a failure. He is Charlotte Brontë's most terrible, most glaring failure. It is not true that Charlotte could not draw men, or that she drew them all alike; Robert Moore, the hard-headed man of business, the man of will and purpose, who never gives up, is not only almost a masterpiece but a spontaneous masterpiece, one of the first examples of his kind. But there is no blood in Louis' veins, no virility in his swarthy body. He is the most unspeakable of schoolmasters. Yet Charlotte lavished on this puppet half the wealth of her imagination. She flings phrase after perfect phrase to him to cover himself with—some of her best things have been given to Louis Moore to utter; but they do not make him live. Again, she strangles him in his own rhetoric. The courtship of Louis Moore and Shirley will not compare with that of Jane and Rochester. There is no nightingale singing in their wood.

Yet, for all that, *Shirley* comes very near to being Charlotte Brontë's masterpiece. It is inspired from first to last with a great intention and a great idea. It shows a vision of reality wider than her grasp. Its faults, like the faults of *Jane Eyre*, are all on the surface, only there is more surface in *Shirley*. If it has not *Jane Eyre's* commanding passion, it has a vaster sweep. It was literally the first attempt in literature to give to woman her right place in the world.

From first to last there is not a page or a line in it that justifies the malignant criticism of Mrs. Oliphant. Caroline Helstone does not justify it. She is no window-gazing virgin on the lookout, in love already before the man has come. She is a young girl, very naturally in love with a man whom she has known for years, who is always on the spot. As for Shirley, she flung herself with all the vehemence of her prophetic soul on the hypocritical convention that would make every woman dependent on some man, and at the same time despises her for the possession of her natural instincts. And Caroline followed her. "I observe that to such grievances as society cannot cure, it usually forbids utterance, on pain of its scorn: this scorn being only a sort of tinselled cloak to its deformed weakness. People hate to be reminded of ills they are unable or unwilling to remedy: such reminder, in forcing on them a sense of their own incapacity, or a more painful sense of an obligation to make some unpleasant effort, troubles their ease and shakes their self-complacency. Old maids, like the houseless and unemployed poor, should not ask for a place and an occupation in the world: the demand disturbs the happy and rich: it disturbs parents.... Men of England! Look at your poor girls, many of them fading round you, dropping off in consumption or decline; or, what is worse, degenerating to sour old maids—envious, back-biting, wretched, because life is a desert to them; or, what is worst of all, reduced to strive, by scarce modest coquetry and debasing artifice, to gain that position and consideration by marriage, which to celibacy is denied. Fathers, cannot you alter these things?... You would wish to be proud of your daughters, and not to blush for them, then seek for them an interest and an occupation which shall raise them above the flirt, the manoeuvrer, the mischief-making talebearer. Keep your girl's minds narrow and degraded—they will still be a plague and a care, sometimes a disgrace to you: give them scope and work—they will be your gayest companions in health; your tenderest nurses in sickness; your most faithful prop in old age."

That is the argument from fathers, and it comes from Caroline Helstone, not from Shirley. And the fact that Caroline married Robert Moore, and Shirley fell in love when her hour came (and with Louis Moore, too!) does not diminish the force or the sincerity or the truth of the tirade.

Shirley may not be a great novel; but it is a great prophetic book. Shirley's vision of the woman kneeling on the hills serves for more than Emily Brontë's vision of Hertha and Demeter, of Eve, the Earth-mother, "the mighty and mystical parent"; it is Charlotte Brontë's vindication of Eve, her vision of woman as she is to be. She faced the world once for all with her vision: "I see her," she said, "and I will tell you what she is like."

Mrs. Oliphant did not see the woman kneeling on the hills. Neither George Eliot nor Mrs. Gaskell saw her. They could not possibly have told the world what she was like. It is part of Charlotte Brontë's superior greatness that she saw.

* * * * *

You do not see that woman in *Villette*. She has passed with the splendour of Charlotte's vision of the world. The world in *Villette* is narrowed to a Pensionnat de Demoiselles, and centred in the heart of one woman. And never, not even in *Jane Eyre*, and certainly not in *Shirley*, did Charlotte Brontë achieve such mastery of reality, and with it such mastery of herself. *Villette* is the final triumph of her genius over the elements that warred in her. It shows the movement of her genius, which was always by impulse and recoil. In *The Professor* she abjured, in the interests of reality, the "imagination" of her youth. In *Jane Eyre* she was urged forward by the released impetus of the forces she repressed. In *Shirley* they are still struggling with her sense of the sober and the sane reality; the book is torn to fragments in the struggle, and in the end imagination riots.

But in *Villette* there are none of these battlings and rendings, these Titanic upheavals and subsidences. Charlotte Brontë's imagination, and her sense of the real, are in process of fusion. There are few novels in which an imagination so supreme is wedded to so vivid a vision of actuality. It may be said that Charlotte Brontë never achieved positive actuality before. The Pensionnat de Demoiselles is almost as visibly and palpably actual as the Maison Vauquer in *Père Goriot*. It is a return to the method of experience with a vengeance. Charlotte's success, indeed, was so stunning that for all but sixty years *Villette* has passed for a *roman à clef*, the novel, not only of experience, but of personal experience. There was a certain plausibility in that view. The characters could all be easily recognized. And when Dr. John was identified with Mr. George Smith, and his mother with Mr. George Smith's mother, and Madame Beck with Madame Héger, and M. Paul Emanuel with Madame Héger's husband, the inference was irresistible: Lucy Snowe was, and could only be, Charlotte Brontë. And as the figure of M. Paul Emanuel was ten times more vivid and convincing than that of Rochester, so all that applied to Jane Eyre applied with ten times more force to Lucy. In *Villette* Charlotte Brontë was considered to have given herself hopelessly away.

I have tried to show that this view cannot stand before an unprejudiced examination of her life and letters. No need to go into all that again. On the evidence, Charlotte seems at the best of times to have fallen in love with difficulty; and she most certainly was no more in love with "the little man", Paul Emanuel, than she was with "the little man", Mr. Taylor. The really important and interesting point is that, if she had been, if he had thus obtained the reality with which passion endows its object, her imagination would have had no use for him; its work would have been done for it.

To the supreme artist the order of the actual event is one thing, and the order of creation is another. Their lines may start from the same point in the actual, they may touch again and again, but they are not the same, and they cannot run exactly parallel. There must always be this difference between the actual thing and the thing drawn from it, however closely, that each is embedded and enmeshed in a different context. For a character in a novel to be alive it must have grown; and to have grown it must have followed its own line of evolution, inevitably and in its own medium; and that, whether or not it has been "taken", as they say, "from life". The more alive it is the less likely is it to have been "taken", to have been seized, hauled by the scruff of its neck out of the dense web of the actual. All that the supreme artist wants is what Charlotte Brontë called "the germ of the real", by which she meant the germ of the actual. He does not want the alien, developed thing, standing in its own medium ready-made. Charlotte Brontë said that the character of Dr. John was a failure because it lacked the germ of the real. She should have said that it lacked the germ of many reals; it is so obviously drawn from incomplete observation of a single instance. I am inclined to think that she did "take" Dr. John. And whenever Charlotte Brontë "took" a character, as she took the unfortunate curates and Mr. St. John Rivers, the result was failure.

No supreme work of art was ever "taken". It was begotten and born and grown, the offspring of faithful love between the soul of the artist and reality. The artist must bring to his "experience" as much as he takes from it. The dignity of Nature is all against these violences and robberies of art. She hides her deepest secret from the marauder, and yields it to the lover who brings to her the fire of his own soul.

And that fire of her own soul was what Charlotte Brontë brought to her supreme creations. It was certainly what she brought to Paul Emanuel. Impossible to believe that M. Héger gave her more than one or two of the germs of M. Paul. Personally, I can only see the respectable M. Héger as a man whose very essence was a certain impassivity and phlegm under the appearance of a temperament. Choleric he was, with the superficial and temporary choler of the schoolmaster. A schoolmaster gifted with the most extraordinary, the most marvellous, the most arresting faculty for making faces, a faculty which in an Englishman would have argued him a perfect volcano of erratic temperament. But I more than suspect that when it came to temperament M. Héger took it out in faces; that he was nothing more than a benevolent, sentimental, passably intellectual bourgeois; but bourgeois to the core. Whereas, look at M. Paul! No wonder that with that tame and solid stuff before her it took even Charlotte Brontë's fiery spirit nine years (torturing the unwilling dross that checked its flight) before it could create Paul Emanuel. Because of her long work on him he is at once the most real and the best imagined of her characters.

I admit that in the drawing of many of her minor characters she seems to have relied upon very close and intimate observation of the living model. But in none of her minor characters is she at grips with the reality that, for her, passion is. Charlotte refused to give heroic rank to persons she had merely observed; she would not exalt them to the dignity of passion. Her imagination could not work on them to that extent. (That is partly why Caroline's delirium is so palpably "faked".) Even in her portrait of the heroic Shirley, who was frankly "taken" from her sister Emily, she achieved the likeness mainly by the artifice of unlikeness, by removing Shirley Keeldar into a life in which Emily Brontë had never played a part, whereby Shirley became for her a separate person. (You cannot by any stretch of the imagination see Emily falling in love with the schoolmaster, Louis Moore.)

Lest there should be any doubt on the subject, Charlotte herself explained to Mrs. Gaskell how her imagination worked. "I asked her," Mrs. Gaskell says, "whether she had ever taken opium, as the description given of its effects in *Villette* was so exactly like what I had experienced—vivid and exaggerated presence of objects, of which the outlines were indistinct, or lost in golden mist, etc. She replied that she had never, to her knowledge, taken a grain of it in any shape, but that she had followed the process she always adopted when she had to describe anything that had not fallen within her own experience; she had thought intently on it for many and many a night before falling asleep—wondering what it was like, or how it would be—till at length, sometimes after her story had been arrested at this one point for weeks, she wakened up in the morning with all clear before her, as if she had in reality gone through the experience, and then could describe it, word for word, as it happened."

To a mind like that the germ of the actual was enough. Charlotte Brontë's genius, in fact, was ardently impatient of the actual: it cared only for its own. At the least hint from experience it was off. A glance, a gesture of M. Héger's was enough to fire it to the conception of Paul Emanuel. He had only to say a kind word to her, to leave a book or a box of bon-bons in her desk (if he *did* leave bon-bons) for Charlotte's fire to work on him. She had only to say to herself, "This little man is adorable in friendship; I wonder what he would be like in love," and she saw that he would be something, though not altogether, like Paul Emanuel. She had only to feel a pang of half-remorseful, half-humorous affection for him, and she knew what Lucy felt like in her love-sick agony. As for Madame Héger, Madame's purely episodic jealousy, her habits of surveillance, her small inscrutabilities of behaviour, became the fury, the treachery, the perfidy of Madame Beck. For treachery and perfidy, and agony and passion, were what Charlotte wanted for *Villette*.

And yet it is true that *Villette* is a novel of experience, owing its conspicuous qualities very much to observation. After all, a contemporary novel cannot be made altogether out of the fire of the great writer's soul. It is because Charlotte Brontë relied too much on the fire of her own soul that in *Jane Eyre* and parts of *Shirley* she missed that unique expression of actuality which, over and over again, she accomplished in *Villette*. For the expression of a social *milieu*, for manners, for the dialogue of ordinary use, for the whole detail of the speech characteristic of an individual and a type, for the right accent and pitch, for all the vanishing shades and aspects of the temporary and the particular, the greatest and the fieriest writer is at the mercy of observation and experience. It was her final mastery of these things that made it possible to praise Charlotte Brontë's powers of observation at the expense of her genius; and this mainly because of M. Paul.

No offspring of genius was ever more alive, more rich in individuality, than M. Paul. He is alive and he is adorable, in his *paletot* and *bonnet grec*, from the moment when he drags Lucy up three pairs of stairs to the solitary and lofty attic and locks her in, to that other moment when he brings her to the little house that he has prepared for her. Whenever he appears there is pure radiant comedy, and pathos as pure. It is in this utter purity, this transparent simplicity, that *Villette* is great. There is not one jarring note in any of the delicious dialogues between Lucy and M. Paul, not one of those passages which must be erased if quotation is not to fail of its effect. Take the scene where Lucy breaks M. Paul's spectacles.

"A score of times ere now I had seen them fall and receive no damage—this time, as Lucy Snowe's hapless luck would have it, they so fell that each clear pebble became a shivered and shapeless star.

"Now, indeed, dismay seized me—dismay and regret. I knew the value of these *lunettes*: M. Paul's sight was peculiar, not easily fitted, and these glasses suited him. I had heard him call them his treasures: as I picked them up, cracked and worthless, my hand trembled. Frightened through all my nerves I was to see the mischief I had done, but I think I was even more sorry than afraid. For some seconds I dared not look the bereaved Professor in the face; he was the first to speak.

"'*Là!*' he said: '*me voilà veuf de mes lunettes*! I think that Mademoiselle Lucy will now confess that the cord and gallows are amply earned; she trembles in anticipation of her doom. Ah, traitress, traitress! You are resolved to have me quite blind and helpless in your hands!'

"I lifted my eyes: his face, instead of being irate, lowering and furrowed, was overflowing with the smile, coloured with the bloom I had seen brightening it that evening at the Hotel Crécy. He was not angry—not even grieved. For the real injury he showed himself full of clemency; under the real provocation, patient as a saint."

Take the "Watchguard" scene.

"M. Paul came and stood behind me. He asked at what I was working; and I said I was making a watchguard. He asked, 'For whom?' And I answered, 'For a gentleman—one of my friends.'"

Whereupon M. Paul flies into a passion, and accuses Lucy of behaving to him, "'With what pungent vivacities—what an impetus of mutiny—what a *fougue* of injustice.'... '*Chut! à l'instant!* There! there I went—*vive comme la poudre.*' He was sorry—he was very sorry: for my sake he grieved over the hopeless peculiarity. This *emportement*, this *chaleur*—generous, perhaps, but excessive—would yet, he feared, do me a mischief. It was a pity. I was not—he believed, in his soul—wholly without good qualities; and would I but hear reason, and be more sedate, more sober, less *en l'air*, less *coquette*, less taken by show, less prone to set an undue value on outside excellence—to make much of the attentions of people remarkable chiefly for so many feet of stature, *des couleurs de poupée, un nez plus ou moins bien fait*, and an enormous amount of fatuity—I might yet prove a useful, perhaps an exemplary character. But, as it was——And here the little man's voice was for a moment choked.

"I would have looked up at him, or held out my hand, or said a soothing word; but I was afraid, if I stirred, I should either laugh or cry; so odd, in all this, was the mixture of the touching and the absurd.

"I thought he had nearly done: but no, he sat down that he might go on at his ease.

"'While he, M. Paul, was on these painful topics, he would dare my anger for the sake of my good, and would venture to refer to a change he had noticed in my dress.'"

* * * * *

"'And if you condemn a bow of ribbon for a lady, monsieur, you would necessarily disapprove of a thing like this for a gentleman?' holding up my bright little chainlet of silk and gold. His sole reply was a groan—I suppose over my levity.

"After sitting some minutes in silence, and watching the progress of the chain, at which I now wrought more assiduously than ever, he inquired:

"'Whether what he had just said would have the effect of making me entirely detest him?'

"I hardly remember what answer I made, or how it came about; I don't think I spoke at all, but I know we managed to bid good night on friendly terms: and even after M. Paul had reached the door, he turned back just to explain that he would not be understood to speak in entire condemnation of the scarlet dress.'...

"'And the flowers under my bonnet, monsieur?' I asked. 'They are very little ones.'

"'Keep them little, then,' said he. 'Permit them not to become full-blown.'

"'And the bow, monsieur—the bit of ribbon?'

"'*Va pour le ruban!*' was the propitious answer.

"And so we settled it."

That is good; and when Lucy presents the watchguard it is better still.

"He looked at the box: I saw its clear and warm tint, and bright azure circlet, pleased his eyes. I told him to open it.

"'My initials!' said he, indicating the letters in the lid. 'Who told you I was called Carl David?'

"'A little bird, monsieur.'

"'Does it fly from me to you? Then one can tie a message under its wing when needful.'

"He took out the chain—a trifle indeed as to value, but glossy with silk and sparkling with beads. He liked that too—admired it artlessly, like a child.

"'For me?'

"'Yes, for you.'

"'This is the thing you were working at last night?'

"'The same.'

"'You finished it this morning?'

"'I did.'

"'You commenced it with the intention that it should be mine?'

"'Undoubtedly.'

"'And offered on my fête-day?'

"'Yes.'

"'This purpose continued as you wove it?'

"'Again I assented.'

"'Then it is not necessary that I should cut out any portion—saying, this part is not mine: it was plaited under the idea and for the adornment of another?'

"'By no means. It is neither necessary, nor would it be just.'

"'This object is *all* mine?'

"'That object is yours entirely.'

"Straightway monsieur opened his paletot, arranged the guard splendidly across his chest, displaying as much and suppressing as little as he could: for he had no notion of concealing what he admired and thought decorative....

"'À present c'est un fait accompli,' said he, readjusting his paletot...."

To the last gesture of Monsieur it is superb.

I have taken those scenes because they are of crucial importance as indications of what Charlotte Brontë was doing in *Villette*, and yet would do. They show not only an enormous advance in technique, but a sense of the situation, of the *scène à faire*, which is entirely or almost entirely lacking in her earlier work.

If there be degrees in reality, Lucy and Pauline de Bassompierre are only less real than M. Paul. And by some miracle their reality is not diminished by Charlotte Brontë's singular change of intention with regard to these two. Little Polly, the child of the beginning, the inscrutable creature of nerves, exquisitely sensitive to pain, fretting her heart out in love for her father and for Graham Bretton, is hardly recognizable in Pauline, Countess de Bassompierre. She has preserved only her fragility, her fastidiousness, her little air of inaccessibility. Polly is obviously predestined to that profound and tragic suffering which is Lucy Snowe's.

"I watched Polly rest her small elbow on her small knee, her head on her hand; I observed her draw a square inch or two of pocket-handkerchief from the doll-pocket of her doll-skirt, and then I heard her weep. Other children in grief or pain cry aloud, without shame or restraint, but this being wept: the tiniest occasional sniff testified to her emotion."

Again (Polly is parted from her father): "When the street-door closed, she dropped on her knees at a chair with a cry—'Papa!'

"It was low and long; a sort of 'why hast thou forsaken me?' During an ensuing space of some minutes I perceived she endured agony. She went through, in that brief interval of her infant life, emotions such as some never feel; it was in her constitution: she would have more of such instants if she lived."

Polly is contrasted with the cold and disagreeable Lucy. "I, Lucy Snowe, was calm," Lucy says when she records that agony. The effect she gives, of something creepily insensitive and most unpleasant, is unmistakable in these early chapters. She watches Polly with a cold, analytic eye. "These sudden, dangerous natures—sensitive as they are called—offer many a curious spectacle to those whom a cooler temperament has secured from participation in their vagaries." When Polly, charming Polly, waits on her father at the tea-table, Lucy is impervious to her tiny charm. "Candidly speaking, I thought her a little busy-body." When Graham Bretton repulses Polly, Lucy has some thoughts of "improving the occasion by inculcating some of those maxims of philosophy whereof I had ever a tolerable stock ready for application."

There is no sign in the beginning that this detestable Lucy is to be heroine. But in Chapter Four Polly disappears and Lucy takes her place and plays her part. The child Polly had a suffering and passionate heart, for all her little air of fastidiousness and inaccessibility. It is the suffering and passionate heart of Polly that beats in Lucy of the Pensionnat. There is only enough of the original Lucy left to sit in judgment on Ginevra Fanshawe and "the Parisienne".

The child Polly had an Imagination. "'Miss Snowe,' said she in a whisper, 'this is a wonderful book ... it tells about distant countries, a long, long way from England, which no traveller can reach without sailing thousands of miles over the sea.... Here is a picture of thousands gathered in a desolate place—a plain spread with sand.... And here are pictures more stranger than that. There is the wonderful Great Wall of China; here is a Chinese lady with a foot littler than mine. There is a wild horse of Tartary; and here—most strange of all—is a land of ice and snow without green fields, woods, or gardens. In this land they found some mammoth bones; there are no mammoths now. You don't know what it was; but I can tell you, because Graham told me. A mighty goblin creature, as high as this room, and as long as the hall; but not a fierce, flesh-eating thing, Graham thinks. He believes if I met one in a forest, it would not kill me, unless I came quite in its way; when it would trample me down amongst the bushes, as I might tread on a grasshopper in a hay-field without knowing it.'"

It is Polly's Imagination that appears again in Lucy's "Creative Impulse". "I with whom that Impulse was the most intractable, the most capricious, the most maddening of masters ... a deity which sometimes, under circumstances apparently propitious, would not speak when questioned, would not hear when appealed to, would not, when sought, be found; but would stand, all cold, all indurated, all granite, a dark Baal with carven lips and blank eyeballs, and breast like the stone face of a tomb; and again, suddenly, at some turn, some sound, some long-trembling sob of the wind, at some rushing past of an unseen stream of electricity, the irrational Demon would awake unsolicited, would stir strangely alive, would rush from its pedestal like a perturbed Dagon, calling to its votary for a sacrifice, whatever the hour—to its victim for some blood or some breath, whatever the circumstances or scene—rousing its priest, treacherously promising vaticination, perhaps filling its temple with a strange hum of oracles, but sure to give half the significance to fateful winds, and grudging to the desperate listener even a miserable remnant—yielding it sordidly, as though each word had been a drop of the deathless ichor of its own dark veins."

That is Lucy. But when Polly reappears fitfully as Pauline de Bassompierre, she is an ordinary, fastidious little lady without a spark of imagination or of passion.

Now in the first three chapters of *Villette*, Charlotte Brontë concentrated all her strength and all her art on the portrait of little Polly. The portrait of little Polly is drawn with the most delicate care and tender comprehension, and the most vivid and entire reality. I cannot agree with Mr. Swinburne that George Eliot, with her Totty and Eppie and Lillo, showed a closer observation of the ways, or a more perfect understanding of the heart of a child. Only little Maggie Tulliver can stand beside little Polly in *Villette*. She is an answer to every critic, from Mr. Swinburne downwards, who maintains that Charlotte Brontë could not draw children.

But Lucy at fourteen is drawn with slight and grudging

strokes, sufficient for the minor part she is evidently to play. Lucy at Bretton is a mere foil to little Polly. Charlotte Brontë distinctly stated in her letters that she did not care for Miss Snowe. "Lucy must not marry Dr. John; he is far too youthful, handsome, bright-spirited, and sweet-tempered; he is a 'curled darling' of Nature and of fortune, and must draw a prize in life's lottery. His wife must be young, rich, pretty; he must be made very happy indeed. If Lucy marries anybody, it must be the Professor—a man in whom there is much to forgive, much to 'put up with'. But I am not leniently disposed towards Miss Frost: from the beginning I never meant to appoint her lines in pleasant places." "As to the character of Lucy Snowe, my intention from the first was that she should not occupy the pedestal to which Jane Eyre was raised by some injudicious admirers. She is where I meant her to be, and where no charge of self-laudation can touch her."

But Lucy is *not* altogether where she was meant to be. When she reappears at the Pensionnat it is with "flame in her soul and lightning in her eyes". She reminds M. Paul "of a young she wild creature, new caught, untamed, viewing with a mixture of fire and fear the first entrance of the breaker-in".

"'You look,' said he, 'like one who would snatch at a draught of sweet poison, and spurn wholesome bitters with disgust.'"

There is no inconsistency in this. Women before now have hidden a soul like a furnace under coldness and unpleasantness, and smothered shrieking nerves under an appearance of apathy. Lucy Snowe is one of them. As far as she goes, Lucy at Bretton is profoundly consistent with Lucy in *Villette*. It is not Lucy's volcanic outbreaks in the Pensionnat that do violence to her creator's original intention. It is the debasement of Polly and the exaltation of Lucy to her tragic rôle, the endowment of Lucy with Polly's rarest qualities, to the utter impoverishment of Pauline de Bassompierre. Polly in *Villette* is a mere foil to Lucy.

Having lavished such care and love on Polly, Charlotte Brontë could not possibly have meant to debase her and efface her. How then did it happen that Polly was debased and Lucy sublimely exalted?

It happened, I think, partly because for the first time Charlotte Brontë created a real living man. The reality of M. Paul Emanuel was too strong both for Lucy and for Charlotte Brontë. From the moment when he seized her and dragged her to the garret he made Lucy live as Charlotte Brontë had never contemplated her living. He made her live to the utter exclusion and extinction of Pauline de Bassompierre.

And "the despotic little man" dominates the book to an extent that Charlotte never contemplated either. Until the storm carried him out of her sight, she was, I think, unaware of his dominion. Dr. John was her hero. She told Mr. George Smith, his prototype, that she intended him for the most beautiful character in the book (which must have been very gratifying to Mr. George Smith). He was the type she needed for her purpose. But he does not "come off", if only for the reason that she is consciously preoccupied with him. Dr. John was far more of an obsession to her than this little man, Paul Emanuel, who was good enough for Lucy Snowe. Pauline de Bassompierre was to be finished and perfected to match the high finish and perfection of Dr. John. Yet neither Pauline nor Dr. John "came off". Charlotte Brontë cared too much for them. But for Paul Emanuel she did not care. He comes off in a triumph of the detached, divinely free "Creative Impulse".

Charlotte, with all her schemes, is delivered over to her genius from the moment when Lucy settles in Villette. To Charlotte's inexperience Brussels was a perfect hotbed for the germs of the real. That, I think, can be admitted without subscribing to the view that it was anything more. Once in the Pensionnat, Lucy entered an atmosphere of the most intense reality. From that point onward the book is literally inspired by the sense of atmosphere, that sense to which experience brings the stuff to work on. All Charlotte's experience and her suffering is there, changed, intensified, transmuted to an experience and a suffering which were not hers.

This matured sense of actuality is shown again in the drawing of the minor characters. There is a certain vindictiveness about the portrait of Ginevra Fanshawe, a touch of that fierce, intolerant temper that caused Blanche Ingram to be strangled by the hands of her creator. Ginevra is not strangled. She lives splendidly; she flourishes in an opulence of detail.

Experience may have partly accounted for Ginevra. It could hardly have accounted for the little de Hamel, and he is perfect as far as he goes.

It is because of this increasing mastery, this new power in handling unsympathetic types, because, in short, of its all round excellence, that *Villette* must count as Charlotte Brontë's masterpiece. It is marvellous that within such limits she should have attained such comparative catholicity of vision. It is not the vast vision of *Shirley*, prophetic and inspired, and a little ineffectual. It is the lucid, sober, unobstructed gaze of a more accomplished artist, the artist whose craving for "reality" is satisfied; the artist who is gradually extending the limits of his art. When Charlotte Brontë wrote *Jane Eyre* she could not appreciate Jane Austen; she wondered why George Henry Lewes liked her so much. She objected to Jane Austen because there was no passion in her, and therefore no poetry and no reality. When she wrote *Shirley* she had seen that passion was not everything; there were other things, very high realities, that were not passion. By the time she wrote *Villette* she saw, not only that there are other things, but that passion is the rarest thing on earth. It does not enter into the life of ordinary people like Dr. John, and Madame Beck, and Ginevra Fanshawe.

In accordance with this tendency to level up, her style in *Villette* attains a more even and a more certain excellence. Her flights are few; so are her lapses. Her fearful tendency to rhetoric is almost gone. Gone too are the purple patches; but there is everywhere delicate colour under a vivid light. But there are countless passages which show the perfection to which she could bring her old imaginative style. Take the scene where Lucy, under the influence of opium, goes into Villette *en fête*.

"The drug wrought. I know not whether Madame had overcharged or under-charged the dose; its result was not that she intended. Instead of stupor, came excitement. I became alive to new thought—to reverie peculiar in colouring. A gathering call ran among the faculties, their bugles sang, their trumpets rang an untimely summons....

"I took a route well known, and went up towards the palatial and royal Haute-Ville; thence the music I heard certainly floated; it was hushed now, but it might rewaken. I went on: neither band nor bell-music came to meet me; another sound replaced it, a sound like a strong tide, a great flow, deepening as I proceeded. Light broke, movement gathered, chimes pealed—to what was I coming? Entering on the level of a Grande Place, I found myself, with the suddenness of magic, plunged amidst a gay, living, joyous crowd.

"Villette is one blaze, one broad illumination; the whole world seems abroad; moonlight and heaven are banished: the town by her own flambeaux, beholds her own splendour—gay dresses, grand equipage, fine horses and gallant riders, throng the bright streets. I see even scores of masks. It is a strange scene, stranger than dreams."

This is only beaten by that lyric passage that ends *Villette*; that sonorous dirge that rings high above all pathos, which is somehow a song of triumph, inspired by the whole power and splendour and magnificence of storm and death.

"The sun passes the equinox; the days shorten, the leaves grow sere; but—he is coming.

"Frosts appear at night; November has sent his fogs in advance; the wind takes its autumn moan; but—he is coming.

"The skies hang full and dark—a rack sails from the west; the clouds cast themselves into strange forms—arches and broad radiations; there rise resplendent mornings—glorious, royal, purple, as monarch in his state; the heavens are one flame; so wild are they, they rival battle at its thickest—so bloody, they shame

Victory in her pride. I know some signs of the sky, I have noted them ever since childhood. God, watch that sail! Oh, guard it!

"The wind shifts to the west. Peace, peace, Banshee—'keening' at every window! It will rise—it will swell—it shrieks out long: wander as I may through the house this night, I cannot lull the blast. The advancing hours make it strong; by midnight all sleepless watchers hear and fear a wild south-west storm.

"That storm roared frenzied for seven days. It did not cease till the Atlantic was strewn with wrecks: it did not lull till the deeps had gorged their fill of substance. Not till the destroying angel of tempest had achieved his perfect work, would he fold the wings whose waft was thunder—the tremor of whose plumes was storm."

* * * * *

After *Villette*, the *Last Sketch*, the *Fragment of Emma*; that fragment which Charlotte Brontë read to her husband not long before her death. All he said was, "The critics will accuse you of repetition."

The critics have fulfilled his cautious prophecy. The *Fragment* passed for one of those sad things of which the least said the better. It was settled that Charlotte Brontë had written herself out, that if she had lived she would have become more and more her own plagiarist. There is a middle-aged lady in *Emma*, presumably conceived on the lines of Mrs. Fairfax and Mrs. Pryor. There is a girls' school, which is only not Lowood because it is so obviously Roe Head or Dewsbury Moor. There is a schoolmistress with sandy hair and thin lips and a cold blue eye, recalling Madame Beck, though there the likeness ceases. And in that school, ill-treated by that schoolmistress, there is a little ugly, suffering, deserted child.

All this looks very much like repetition. But it does not shake my private belief that *Emma* is a fragment of what would have been as great a novel as *Villette*. There are indications. There is

Mr. Ellin, who proves that Charlotte Brontë could create a live man of the finer sort, an unexploited masculine type with no earthly resemblance to Rochester or to Louis Moore or M. Paul. He is an unfinished sketch rather than a portrait, but a sketch that would not too shamefully have discredited Mr. Henry James. For there is a most modern fineness and subtlety in *Emma*; and, for all its sketchy incompleteness, a peculiar certainty of touch, an infallible sense of the significant action, the revealing gesture. With a splendid economy of means, scenes, passages, phrases, apparently slight, are charged with the most intense psychological suggestion. When Mr. Ellin, summoned on urgent business by Miss Wilcox, takes that preposterously long and leisurely round to get to her, you know what is passing in the mind of Mr. Ellin as well as if you had been told. In that brief scene between Mr. Ellin and the schoolmistress, you know as well as if you had been told, that Miss Wilcox has lost Mr. Ellin because of her unkindness to a child. When the child, Matilda Fitzgibbon, falls senseless, and Mr. Ellin gives his inarticulate cry and lifts her from the floor, the enigmatic man has revealed his innermost nature.

Now a fragment that can suggest all this with the smallest possible expenditure of phrases, is not a fragment that can be set aside. It is slight; but slightness that accomplishes so much is a sign of progress rather than of falling-off. We shall never know what happened to Matilda when Mr. Ellin took her from Miss Wilcox. We shall never know what happened to Mr. Ellin; but I confess that I am dying to know, and that I find it hard to forgive Mr. Nicholls for having killed them, so certain am I that they would have lived triumphantly if Charlotte Brontë had not married him.

Some of us will be profoundly indifferent to this issue; for Charlotte Brontë has no following in a certain school. She defies analysis. You cannot label her. What she has done is not "Realism", neither is it "Romance". She displeases both by her ambiguity and by her lack of form. She has no infallible dramatic instinct. Even in *Villette* she preserves some of her clumsiness, her crudity, her improbability. The progress of "the Novel" in our day is towards a perfection of form and a reality she never knew.

But "reality" is a large term; and, as for form, *who* cared about it in the fifties? As for improbability—as M. Dimnet says—she is not more improbable than Balzac.

And all these things, the ambiguity, the formlessness and the rest, she was gradually correcting as she advanced. It is impossible to exaggerate the importance and significance of her attainment in *Villette*; there has been so much confused thinking in the consecrated judgment of that novel. *Villette* owes its high place largely to its superior construction and technique; largely and primarily to Charlotte Brontë's progress towards the light, towards the world, towards the great undecorated reality. It is odd criticism that ignores the inevitable growth, the increasing vision and grasp, the whole indomitable advance of a great writer, and credits "experience" with the final masterpiece. As a result of this confusion *Villette* has been judged "final" in another sense. Yes, final—this novel that shows every sign and token of long maturing, long-enduring power. If Charlotte Brontë's critics had not hypnotized themselves by the perpetual reiteration of that word "experience", it would have been impossible for them, with the evidence of her work before them, to have believed that in *Villette* she had written herself out.

She was only just beginning.

* * * * *

Of Charlotte Brontë's *Poems* there is not much to say. They are better poems than Branwell's or Anne's, but that does not make them very good. Still, they are interesting, and they are important, because they are the bridge by which Charlotte Brontë passed into her own dominion. She took Wordsworth with his Poems and Ballads for her guide, and he misled her and delayed her on her way, and kept her a long time standing on her bridge. For in her novels, and her novels only, Charlotte was a poet. In her poems she is a novelist, striving and struggling for expression in a cramped form, an imperfect and improper medium. But most indubitably a novelist. Nearly all her poems which are not artificial are impersonal. They deal with "situations", with "psychological problems", that cry aloud for prose. There is the "Wife" who seems to have lived a long, adventurous life with "William" through many poems; there is the deserted wife and mother in "Mementos"; there is "Frances", the deserted maiden; there is "Gilbert" with his guilty secret and his suicide, a triple domestic tragedy in the three acts of a three-part ballad; there is the lady in "Preference", who prefers her husband to her passionate and profoundly deluded lover; there is the woman in "Apostasy", wrecked in the conflict between love and priestcraft; and there is little else beside. These poems are straws, showing the way of the wind that bloweth where it listeth.

* * * * *

Too much has been written about Charlotte Brontë, and far too much has been read. You come away from it with an enormous mass of printed stuff wrecked in your memory, letters, simply hundreds of letters, legends and theories huddled together in a heap, with all values and proportions lost; and your impression is of tumult and of suffering, and of a multitude of confused and incongruous happenings; funerals and flirtations, or something very like flirtations, to the sound of the passing bell and sexton's chisel; upheavals of soul, flights to and from Brussels, interminable years of exile, and of lurid, tragic passion; years, interminable, monotonous years of potato-peeling and all manner of household piety; scenes of debauchery, horrors of opium and of drink; celebrity, cataclysmal celebrity, rushings up to town in storm and darkness, dim coffee-houses in Paternoster Row, dinner-parties; deaths, funerals, melancholia; and still celebrity; years, interminable, monotonous years of blazing celebrity, sounds of the literary workshop overpowering the sexton's chisel; then marriage, sudden and swift; then death. And in the midst of it all, one small and rather absurd and obscure figure, tossed to and fro, said to be Charlotte Brontë.

What an existence!

This is the impression created by the bibliographical total. But sweep four-fifths of it away, all the legends and half the letters, and sort and set out what remains, observing values and proportions, and you get an outer life where no great and moving event ever came, saving only death (Charlotte's marriage hardly counts beside it); an outer life of a strange and almost oppressive simplicity and silence; and an inner life, tumultuous and profound in suffering, a life to all appearances frustrate, where all nourishment of the emotions was reduced to the barest allowance a woman's heart can depend on and yet live; and none the less a life that out of that starvation diet raised enough of rich and vivid and superb emotion to decorate a hundred women's lives; an inner life which her genius fed and was fed from, for which no reality, no experience, could touch its own intensity of realization. And, genius apart, in the region of actual and ostensible emotion, no one of us can measure the depth of her adoration of duty, or the depth, the force and volume of her passion for her own people, and for the earth trodden by their feet, the earth that covered them. Beside it every other feeling was temporary and insignificant. In the light of it you see Charlotte Brontë's figure for ever simple and beautiful and great; behind her for ever the black-grey setting of her village and the purple of her moors. That greatness and beauty and simplicity is destroyed by any effort to detach her from her background. She may seem susceptible to the alien influences of exile; but it is as an exile that she suffers; and her most inspired moments are her moments of return, when she wrote prose like this: "The moon reigns glorious, glad of the gale; as glad as if she gave herself to his fierce caress with love. No Endymion will watch for his goddess to-night: there are no flocks on the mountains."

* * * * *

Around the figure of Emily Brontë there is none of that clamour and confusion. She stands apart in an enduring silence, and guards for ever her secret and her mystery. By the mercy of heaven the swarm of gossips and of theorists has passed her by. She has no legend or hardly any. So completely has she been passed over that when Madame Duclaux came to write the Life of Emily Brontë she found little to add to Mrs. Gaskell's meagre record beyond that story, which she tells with an incomparable simplicity and reticence, of Emily in her mortal illness, sitting by the hearth, combing her long hair till the comb slips from her fingers.

That is worth all the reams, the terrible reams that have been written about Charlotte.

There can be no doubt that Emily Brontë found her shelter behind Charlotte's fame; but she was protected most of all by the unapproachable, the unique and baffling quality of her temperament and of her genius. Her own people seem to have felt it; Charlotte herself in that preface to *Wuthering Heights*, which stands as her last vindication and eulogy of her dead sister, even Charlotte betrays a curious reservation and reluctance. You feel that Emily's genius inspired her with a kind of sacred terror.

Charlotte destroyed all records of her sister except her poems. Between six and seven hundred of her own letters have been published; there are two of Emily's. They tell little or nothing. And there was that diary she kept for Anne, where she notes with extreme brevity the things that are happening in her family. There never was a diary wherein the soul of the diarist was so well concealed.

And yet, because of this silence, this absence of legend and conjecture, we see Emily Brontë more clearly than we can ever hope to see Charlotte now. Though hardly anything is known of her, what *is* known is authentic; it comes straight from those who knew and loved her: from Charlotte, from Ellen Nussey, from the servants at the Parsonage. Even of her outward and visible presence we have a clearer image. The lines are fewer, but they are more vivid. You see her tall and slender, in her rough clothes, tramping the moors with the form and the step of a virile adolescent. Shirley, the "*bête fauve*", is Emily civilized. You see her head carried high and crowned with its long, dark hair, coiled simply, caught up with a comb. You see her face, honey-pale, her slightly high, slightly aquiline nose; her beautiful eyes, dark-grey, luminous; the "kind, kindling, liquid eyes" that Ellen Nussey saw; and their look, one moment alert, intent, and the next, inaccessibly remote.

I have seen such kind and kindling eyes in the face of a visionary, born with a profound, incurable indifference to the material event; for whom the Real is the incredible, unapparent harmony that flows above, beneath, and within the gross flux of appearances. To him it is the sole thing real. That kind and kindling look I know to be simply a light reflected from the surface of the dream. It is anything but cold; it has indeed a certain tender flame; but you would be profoundly mistaken if you argued from it more than the faintest polite interest in you and your affairs. The kindling of Emily Brontë's eyes I take to have had at times something of the same unearthly quality. Strangers received from her an impression as of a creature utterly removed from them; a remoteness scarcely human, hard to reconcile with her known tenderness for every living thing. She seems to have had a passionate repugnance to alien and external contacts, and to have felt no more than an almost reluctant liking for the lovable and charming Ellen Nussey. Indeed, she regarded Charlotte's friend with the large and virile tolerance that refuses to be charmed.

And yet in the depths of her virginal nature there was something fiercely tender and maternal. There can be no doubt that she cared for Charlotte, who called her "Mine own bonnie love"; but she would seem to have cared far more for Anne who was young and helpless, and for Branwell who was helpless and most weak.

Thus there is absolutely nothing known of Emily that destroys or disturbs the image that Haworth holds of her; nothing that detaches her for a moment from her own people, and from her own place. Her days of exile count not at all in her thirty years of home. No separation ever broke, for one hour that counted, the bonds that bound her to her moors, or frustrated the divine passion of her communion with their earth and sky. Better still, no tale of passion such as they tell of Charlotte was ever told of Emily.

It may be told yet, for no secret thing belonging to this disastrous family is sacred. There may be somewhere some awful worshipper of Emily Brontë, impatient of her silence and unsatisfied with her strange, her virgin and inaccessible beauty, who will some day make up a story of some love-affair, some passion kindred to Catherine Earnshaw's passion for Heathcliff, of which her moors have kept the secret; and he will tell his tale. But we shall at least know that he had made it up. And even so, it will have been better for that man if he had never been born. He will have done his best to destroy or to deface the loveliness of a figure unique in literature. And he will have ignored the one perfect, the one essentially true picture of Emily Brontë, which is to be found in Maurice Maeterlinck's *Wisdom and Destiny*.

To M. Maeterlinck she is the supreme instance of the self-sufficing soul, independent and regardless of the material event. She shows the emptiness, the impotence, the insignificance of all that we call "experience," beside the spirit that endures. "Not a single event ever paused as it passed by her threshold; yet did every event she could claim take place in her heart, with incomparable force and beauty, with matchless precision and detail. We say that nothing ever happened; but did not all things really happen to her much more directly and tangibly than with most of us, seeing that everything that took place about her, everything that she saw or heard was transformed within her into thoughts and feelings, into indulgent love, admiration, adoration of life...?

"Of her happiness none can doubt. Not in the soul of the best of all those whose happiness has lasted longest, been the most active, diversified, perfect, could more imperishable harvest be found, than in the soul Emily Brontë lays bare. If to her there came nothing of all that passes in love, sorrow, passion or anguish, still did she possess all that abides when emotion has faded away."[A]

[Footnote A: *Wisdom and Destiny*, translated by Alfred Sutro.]

What was true of Charlotte, that her inner life was luminous with intense realization, was a hundred times more true of Emily. It was so true that beside it nothing else that can be said is altogether true. It is not necessary for a man to be convinced of the illusory nature of time and of material happenings in order to appreciate Charlotte's genius; but his comprehension of Emily's will be adequate or otherwise, according to the passion and sincerity with which he embraces that idea. And he must have, further, a sense of the reality behind the illusion. It is through her undying sense of it that Emily Brontë is great. She had none of the proud appearances of the metaphysical mind; she did not, so far as we know, devour, like George Eliot, whole systems of philosophy in her early youth. Her passionate pantheism was not derived; it was established in her own soul. She was a mystic, not by religious vocation, but by temperament and by ultimate vision. She offers the apparent anomaly of extreme detachment and of an unconquerable love of life.

It was the highest and the purest passion that you can well conceive. For life gave her nothing in return. It treated her worse than it treated Charlotte. She had none of the things that, after all, Charlotte had; neither praise nor fame in her lifetime; nor friendship, nor love, nor vision of love. All these things "passed her by with averted head"; and she stood in her inviolable serenity and watched them go, without putting out her hand to one of them. You cannot surprise her in any piteous gesture of desire or regret. And, unlike Charlotte, she made it impossible for you to pity her.

It is this superb attitude to life, this independence of the material event, this detachment from the stream of circumstance, that marks her from her sister; for Charlotte is at moments pitifully immersed in the stream of circumstance, pitifully dependent on the material event. It is true that she kept her head above the stream, and that the failure of the material event did not frustrate or hinder her ultimate achievement. But Charlotte's was not by any means "a chainless soul". It struggled and hankered after the unattainable. What she attained and realized she realized and attained in her imagination only. She knew nothing of the soul's more secret and intimate possession. And even her imagination waited to some extent upon experience. When Charlotte wrote of passion, of its tragic suffering, or of its ultimate appeasing, she, after all, wrote of things that might have happened to her. But when Emily wrote of passion, she wrote of a thing that, so far as she personally was concerned, not only was not and had not been, but never could be. It was true enough of Charlotte that she created. But of Emily it was absolutely and supremely true.

Hers is not the language of frustration, but of complete and satisfying possession. It may seem marvellous in the mouth of a woman destitute of all emotional experience, in the restricted sense; but the real wonder would have been a *Wuthering Heights* born of any personal emotion; so certain is it that it was through her personal destitution that her genius was so virile and so rich. At its hour it found her virgin, not only to passion but to the bare idea of passion, to the inner and immaterial event.

And her genius was great, not only through her stupendous imagination, but because it fed on the still more withdrawn and secret sources of her soul. If she had had no genius she would yet be great because of what took place within her, the fusion of her soul with the transcendent and enduring life.

It was there that, possessing nothing, she possessed all things; and her secret escapes you if you are aware only of her splendid paganism. She never speaks the language of religious resignation like Anne and Charlotte. It is most unlikely that she relied, openly or in secret, on "the merits of the Redeemer", or on any of the familiar consolations of religion. As she bowed to no disaster and no grief, consolation would have been the last thing in any religion that she looked for. But, for height and depth of supernatural attainment, there is no comparison between Emily's grip of divine reality and poor Anne's spasmodic and despairing clutch; and none between Charlotte's piety, her "God willing"; "I suppose I ought to be thankful", and Emily's acceptance and endurance of the event.

I am reminded that one event she neither accepted nor endured. She fought death. Her spirit lifted the pathetic, febrile struggle of weakness with corruption, and turned it to a splendid, Titanic, and unearthly combat.

And yet it was in her life rather than her death that she was splendid. There is something shocking and repellent in her last defiance. It shrieks discord with the endurance and acceptance, braver than all revolt, finer than all resignation, that was the secret of her genius and of her life.

There is no need to reconcile this supreme detachment with the storm and agony that rages through *Wuthering Heights*, or with the passion for life and adoration of the earth that burns there, an imperishable flame; or with Catherine Earnshaw's dream of heaven: "heaven did not seem to be my home; and I broke my heart with weeping to come back to earth; and the angels were so angry that they flung me out into the middle of the heath on the top of Wuthering Heights; where I woke sobbing for joy". Catherine Earnshaw's dream has been cited innumerable times to prove that Emily Brontë was a splendid pagan. I do not know what it does prove, if it is not the absolute and immeasurable greatness of her genius, that, dwelling as she undoubtedly did dwell, in the secret and invisible world, she could yet conceive and bring forth Catherine Earnshaw.

It is not possible to diminish the force or to take away one word of Mr. Swinburne's magnificent eulogy. There *was* in the "passionate great genius of Emily Brontë", "a dark, unconscious instinct as of primitive nature-worship". That was where she was so poised and so complete; that she touches earth and heaven, and is at once intoxicated with the splendour of the passion of living, and holds her spirit in security and her heart in peace. She plunged with Catherine Earnshaw into the thick of the tumult, and her detachment is not more wonderful than her immersion.

It is our own imperfect vision that is bewildered by the union in her of these antagonistic attitudes. It is not only entirely possible and compatible, but, if your soul be comprehensive, it is inevitable that you should adore the forms of life, and yet be aware of their impermanence; that you should affirm with equal fervour their illusion and the radiance of the reality that manifests itself in them. Emily Brontë was nothing if not comprehensive. There was no distance, no abyss too vast, no antagonism, no contradiction too violent and appalling for her embracing soul. Without a hint, so far as we know, from any philosophy, by a sheer flash of genius she pierced to the secret of the world and crystallized it in two lines:

> The earth that wakes *one* human heart to feeling
> Can centre both the worlds of Heaven and Hell.

It is doubtful if she ever read a line of Blake; yet it is Blake that her poems perpetually recall, and it is Blake's vision that she has reached there. She too knew what it was

> To see a world in a grain of sand,
>   And a Heaven in a wild flower,
> To hold Infinity in the palm of your hand,
>   And Eternity in an hour.

She sees by a flash what he saw continuously; but it is by the same light she sees it and wins her place among the mystics.

Her mind was not always poised. It swung between its vision of transparent unity and its love of earth for earth's sake. There are at least four poems of hers that show this entirely natural oscillation.

In one, a nameless poem, the Genius of Earth calls to the visionary soul:

> Shall earth no more inspire thee,
>   Thou lonely dreamer now?
> Since passion may not fire thee,
>   Shall nature cease to bow?
>
> Thy mind is ever moving
>   In regions dark to thee;
> Recall its useless roving,
>   Come back, and dwell with me.

* * * * *

> Few hearts to mortals given
>   On earth so wildly pine;
> Yet few would ask a heaven
>   More like this earth than thine.

"The Night-Wind" sings the same song, lures with the same enchantment; and the human voice answers, resisting:

> Play with the scented flower,
>   The young tree's supple bough,
> And leave my human feelings
>   In their own course to flow.

But the other voice is stronger:

> The wanderer would not heed me;
>   Its kiss grew warmer still.
> "Oh, come," it sighed so sweetly;
>   "I'll win thee 'gainst thy will.
>
> "Were we not friends from childhood?
>   Have I not loved thee long?
> As long as thou, the solemn night,
>   Whose silence wakes my song.
>
> "And when thy heart is resting
>   Beneath the church-aisle stone,
> *I* shall have time for mourning,
>   And *thou* for being alone."

There are nine verses of "The Night-Wind", and the first eight are negligible; but, as for the last and ninth, I do not know any poem in any language that renders, in four short lines, and with such incomparable magic and poignancy, the haunting and pursuing of the human by the inhuman, that passion of the homeless and eternal wind.

And this woman, destitute, so far as can be known, of all metaphysical knowledge or training, reared in the narrowest and least metaphysical of creeds, did yet contrive to express in one poem of four irregular verses all the hunger and thirst after the "Absolute" that ever moved a human soul, all the bewilderment and agony inflicted by the unintelligible spectacle of existence, the intolerable triumph of evil over good, and did conceive an image and a vision of the transcendent reality that holds, as in crystal, all the philosophies that were ever worthy of the name.

Here it is. There are once more two voices: one of the Man, the other of the Seer:

THE PHILOSOPHER

Oh, for the time when I shall sleep
  Without identity.
And never care how rain may steep,
  Or snow may cover me!
No promised heaven, these wild desires
  Could all, or half fulfil;
No threatened hell, with quenchless fires,
  Subdue this restless will.

So said I, and still say the same;
  Still, to my death, will say—
Three gods, within this little frame,
  Are warring night and day;
Heaven could not hold them all, and yet
  They all are held in me;
And must be mine till I forget
  My present entity!
Oh, for the time, when in my breast
  Their struggles will be o'er!
Oh, for the day, when I shall rest,
  And never suffer more!

I saw a spirit, standing, man,
  Where thou dost stand—an hour ago,
And round his feet three rivers ran,
  Of equal depth, and equal flow—
A golden stream—and one like blood,
  And one like sapphire seemed to be;
But where they joined their triple flood
  It tumbled in an inky sea.
The spirit sent his dazzling gaze
  Down through that ocean's gloomy night;

> Then, kindling all, with sudden blaze,—
> The glad deep sparkled wide and bright—
> White as the sun, far, far more fair
> Than its divided sources were!
>
> And even for that spirit, seer,
>   I've watched and sought my lifetime long;
> Sought him in heaven, hell, earth and air,
>   An endless search and always wrong.
> Had I but seen his glorious eye
>   *Once* light the clouds that 'wilder me,
> I ne'er had raised this coward cry
>   To cease to think, and cease to be;
> I ne'er had called oblivion blest,
>   Nor, stretching eager hands to death,
> Implored to change for senseless rest
>   This sentient soul, this living breath—
> Oh, let me die—that power and will
>   Their cruel strife may close,
> And conquered good and conquering ill
>   Be lost in one repose!

That vision of the transcendent spirit, with the mingled triple flood of life about his feet, is one that Blake might have seen and sung and painted.

The fourth poem, "The Prisoner", is a fragment, and an obscure fragment, which may belong to a very different cycle. But whatever its place, it has the same visionary quality. The vision is of the woman captive, "confined in triple walls", the "guest darkly lodged", the "chainless soul", that defies its conqueror, its gaoler, and the spectator of its agony. It has, this prisoner, its own unspeakable consolation, the "Messenger":

> He comes with western winds, with evening's wandering
> airs,

> With that clear dusk of heaven that brings the thickest stars.
> Winds take a pensive tone, and stars a tender fire,
> And visions rise and change that kill me with desire.

* * * * *

> But, first, a hush of peace—a soundless calm descends;
> The struggle of distress, and fierce impatience ends;
> Mute music soothes my breast—unuttered harmony,
> That I could never dream, till earth was lost to me.
>
> Then dawns the Invisible; the Unseen its truth reveals;
> My outward sense is gone, my inward essence feels:
> Its wings are almost free—its home, its harbour found,
> Measuring the gulf, it stoops and dares the final bound.

That is the language of a mystic, of a mystic who has passed beyond contemplation; who has known or imagined ecstasy. The joy is unmistakable; unmistakable, too, is the horror of the return:

> Oh! dreadful is the check—intense the agony—
> When the ear begins to hear, and the eye begins to see;
> When the pulse begins to throb, the brain to think again;
> The soul to feel the flesh, and the flesh to feel the chain.

There is no doubt about those three verses; that they are the expression of the rarest and the most tremendous experience that is given to humanity to know.

If "The Visionary" does not touch that supernal place, it belongs indubitably to the borderland:

Silent is the house; all are laid asleep:
One alone looks out o'er the snow-wreaths deep,
Watching every cloud, dreading every breeze
That whirls the wildering drift and bends the groaning trees.

Cheerful is the hearth, soft the matted floor;
Not one shivering gust creeps through pane or door;
The little lamp burns straight, the rays shoot strong and far
I trim it well to be the wanderer's guiding-star.

Frown, my haughty sire! chide, my angry dame!
Set your slaves to spy; threaten me with shame;
But neither sire nor dame, nor prying serf shall know,
What angel nightly tracks that waste of frozen snow.

What I love shall come like visitant of air,
Safe in secret power from lurking human snare;
What loves me no word of mine shall e'er betray,
Though for faith unstained my life must forfeit pay.

Burn then, little lamp; glimmer straight and clear—
Hush! a rustling wing stirs, methinks, the air;
He for whom I wait, thus ever comes to me:
Strange Power! I trust thy might; trust thou my constancy.

Those who can see nothing in this poem but the idealization of an earthly passion must be strangely and perversely mistaken in their Emily Brontë. I confess I can never read it without thinking of one of the most marvellous of all poems of Divine Love: "En una Noche Escura".

EN UNA NOCHE ESCURA[A]

Upon an obscure night
Fevered with Love's anxiety
(O hapless, happy plight!)
I went, none seeing me,
Forth from my house, where all things quiet be.

* * * * *

Blest night of wandering
In secret, when by none might I be spied,
Nor I see anything;
Without a light to guide
Save that which in my heart burnt in my side.

That light did lead me on
More surely than the shining of noontide,
Where well I knew that One
Did for my coming bide;
Where he abode might none but he abide.

O night that didst lead thus;
O night more lovely than the dawn of light;
O night that broughtest us
Lover to lover's sight,
Lover to loved, in marriage of delight!

[Footnote A: "St. John of the Cross: The Dark Night of the Soul." Translated by Arthur Symons in vol. ii. of his *Collected Poems*.]

THE THREE BRONTËS

* * * * *

We know what love is celebrated there, and we do not know so clearly what manner of supernal passion is symbolized in Emily Brontë's angel-lover. There is a long way there between Emily Brontë and St. John of the Cross, between her lamp-lit window and his "Dark Night of the Soul", and yet her opening lines have something of the premonitory thrill, the haunting power of tremendous suggestion, the intense, mysterious expectancy of his. The spiritual experience is somewhat different, but it belongs to the same realm of the super-physical; and it is very far from Paganism.

She wrote of these supreme ardours and mysteries; and she wrote that most inspired and vehement song of passionate human love, "Remembrance":

> Cold in the earth—and the deep snow piled above thee,
> Far, far removed, cold in the dreary grave!
> Have I forgot, my only Love, to love thee....

But "Remembrance" is too well known for quotation here. So is "The Old Stoic".

These are perfect and unforgettable things. But there is hardly one of the least admirable of her poems that has not in it some unforgettable and perfect verse or line:

> And oh, how slow that keen-eyed star
>   Has tracked the chilly grey!
> What, watching yet? how very far
>   The morning lies away.

That is how some watcher on Wuthering Heights might measure the long passage of the night.

"The Lady to her Guitar", that recalls the dead and forgotten player, sings:

> It is as if the glassy brook
>   Should image still its willows fair,
> *Though years ago the woodman's stroke*
> *Laid low in dust their Dryad-hair.*

She has her "dim moon struggling in the sky", to match Charlotte's "the moon reigns glorious, glad of the gale, glad as if she gave herself to his fierce caress with love". At sixteen, in the schoolroom,[A] she wrote verses of an incomparable simplicity and poignancy:

> A little while, a little while,
>   The weary task is put away,
> And I can sing and I can smile,
>   Alike, while I have holiday.
>
> Where wilt thou go, my harassed heart—
>   What thought, what scene invites thee now?
> What spot, or near or far apart,
>   Has rest for thee, my weary brow?

* * * * *

> The house is old, the trees are bare,
>   Moonless above bends twilight's dome;
> But what on earth is half so dear—
>   So longed for—as the hearth of home?
>
> The mute bird sitting on the stone,
>   The dank moss dripping from the wall,
> The thorn-trees gaunt, the walks o'ergrown,
>   I love them—how I love them all!

Still, as I mused, the naked room,
  The alien firelight died away,
And, from the midst of cheerless gloom,
  I passed to bright, unclouded day.

A little and a lone green lane
  That opened on a common wide;
A distant, dreamy, dim blue chain
  Of mountains circling every side.

A heaven so clear, an earth so calm.
  So sweet, so soft, so hushed an air;
And, deepening still the dream-like charm,
  Wild moor-sheep feeding everywhere.

[Footnote A: Madame Duclaux assigns to these verses a much later date—the year of Emily Brontë's exile in Brussels. Sir William Robertson Nicoll also considers that "the 'alien firelight' suits Brussels better than the Yorkshire hearth of 'good, kind' Miss Wooler". To me the schoolroom of the Pensionnat suggests an "alien" stove, and not the light of any fire at all.]

* * * * *

There was no nostalgia that she did not know. And there was no funeral note she did not sound; from the hopeless gloom of

In the earth—the earth—thou shalt be laid,
  A grey stone standing over thee;
Black mould beneath thee spread,
  And black mould to cover thee.

Well—there is rest there,
  So fast come thy prophecy;

The time when my sunny hair
  Shall with grass-roots entwined be.

But cold—cold is that resting-place
  Shut out from joy and liberty,
And all who loved thy living face
  Will shrink from it shudderingly.

From that to the melancholy grace of the moorland dirge:

The linnet in the rocky dells,
  The moor-lark in the air,
The bee among the heather-bells
  That hide my lady fair:

The wild deer browse above her breast;
  The wild birds raise their brood;
And they, her smiles of love caressed,
  Have left her solitude.

* * * * *

Well, let them fight for honour's breath,
  Or pleasure's shade pursue—
The dweller in the land of death
  Is changed and careless too.

And if their eyes should watch and weep
  Till sorrow's source were dry,
She would not, in her tranquil sleep,
  Return a single sigh.

> Blow, west wind, by the lowly mound,
>   And murmur, summer-streams—
> There is no need of other sound
>   To soothe my lady's dreams.

There is, finally, that nameless poem—her last—where Emily Brontë's creed finds utterance. It also is well known, but I give it here by way of justification, lest I should seem to have exaggerated the mystic detachment of this lover of the earth:

> No coward soul is mine,
> No trembler in the world's storm-troubled sphere:
>   I see Heaven's glories shine,
>   And faith shines equal, arming me from fear.
>
>   O God within my breast,
> Almighty, ever-present Deity!
>   Life—that in me has rest,
> As I—undying Life—have power in thee!
>
>   Vain are the thousand creeds
> That move men's hearts: unutterably vain;
>   Worthless as withered weeds,
> Or idlest froth amid the boundless main.
>
>   To waken doubt in one
> Holding so fast by thine infinity;
>   So surely anchored on
> The steadfast rock of immortality.
>
>   With wide-embracing love
> Thy spirit animates eternal years,
>   Pervades and broods above,
> Changes, sustains, dissolves, creates, and rears.

> Though earth and man were gone,
> And suns and universes ceased to be,
> And Thou wert left alone,
> Every existence would exist in Thee.
>
> There is not room for Death,
> Nor atom that his might could render void:
> Thou—THOU art Being and Breath,
> And what THOU art may never be destroyed.

It is not a perfect work. I do not think it is by any means the finest poem that Emily Brontë ever wrote. It has least of her matchless, incommunicable quality. There is one verse, the fifth, that recalls almost painfully the frigid poets of Deism of the eighteenth century. But even that association cannot destroy or contaminate its superb sincerity and dignity. If it recalls the poets of Deism, it recalls no less one of the most ancient of all metaphysical poems, the poem of Parmenides on Being:
[Greek: pos d' an epeit apoloito pelon, pos d' an ke genoito; ei ge genoit, ouk est', oud ei pote mellei esesthai.

* * * * *

tos, genesis men apesbestai kai apiotos olethros.
oude diaireton estin, epei pan estin homoion
oude ti pae keneon....
      ....eon gar eonti pelazei.]

Parmenides had not, I imagine, "penetrated" to Haworth; yet the last verse of Emily Brontë's poem might have come straight out of his [Greek: ta pros halaetheiaen]. Truly, an astonishing poem to have come from a girl in a country parsonage in the 'forties.

But the most astonishing thing about it is its inversion of a yet more consecrated form: "Thou hast made us for Thyself, and our hearts are restless till they rest in Thee". Emily Brontë does not follow St. Augustine. She has an absolutely inspired and independent insight:

> Life—that in me has rest,
> As I—undying Life—have power in Thee!

For there was but little humility or resignation about Emily Brontë. Nothing could be prouder than her rejection of the view that must have been offered to her every Sunday from her father's pulpit. She could not accept the Christian idea of separation and the Mediator. She knew too well the secret. She saw too clearly the heavenly side of the eternal quest. She heard, across the worlds, the downward and the upward rush of the Two immortally desirous; when her soul cried she heard the answering cry of the divine pursuer: "My heart is restless till it rests in Thee." It is in keeping with her vision of the descent of the Invisible, who comes

With that clear dusk of heaven that brings the thickest stars,

her vision of the lamp-lit window, and the secret, unearthly consummation.

There is no doubt about it. And there is no doubt about the Paganism either. It seems at times the most apparent thing about Emily Brontë.

The truth is that she revealed her innermost and unapparent nature only in her poems. That was probably why she was so annoyed when Charlotte discovered them.

* * * * *

Until less than ten years ago it was commonly supposed that Charlotte had discovered all there were. Then sixty-seven hitherto unpublished poems appeared in America. And the world went on unaware of what had happened.

And now Mr. Clement Shorter, in his indefatigable researches, has unearthed seventy-one more, and published them with the sixty-seven and with Charlotte's thirty-nine.[A]

[Footnote A: *Complete Works of Emily Brontë*. Vol. I.—Poetry. (Messrs. Hodder and Stoughton, 1910.)]

And the world continues more or less unaware.

I do not know how many new poets Vigo Street can turn out in a week. But I do know that somehow the world is made sufficiently aware of some of them. But this event, in which Vigo Street has had no hand, the publication, after more than sixty years, of the Complete Poems of Emily Brontë, has not, so far as I know, provoked any furious tumult of acclaim.

And yet there could hardly well have been an event of more importance in its way. If the best poems in Mr. Shorter's collection cannot stand beside the best in Charlotte's editions of 1846 and 1850, many of them reveal an aspect of Emily Brontë's genius hitherto unknown and undreamed of; one or two even reveal a little more of the soul of Emily Brontë than has yet been known.

There are no doubt many reasons for the world's indifference. The few people in it who read poetry at all do not read Emily Brontë much; it is as much as they can do to keep pace with the perpetual, swift procession of young poets out of Vigo Street. There is a certain austerity about Emily Brontë, a superb refusal of all extravagance, pomp, and decoration, which makes her verses look naked to eyes accustomed to young lyrics loaded with "jewels five-words long". About Emily Brontë there is no emerald and beryl and chrysoprase; there are no vine-leaves in her hair, and on her white Oread's feet there is no stain of purple vintage. She knows nothing of the Dionysiac rapture and the sensuous side of mysticism. She can give nothing to the young soul that thirsts and hungers for these things.

It is not surprising, therefore, that the world should be callous to Emily Brontë. What you are not prepared for is the appearance of indifference in her editors. They are pledged by their office to a peculiar devotion. And the circumstances of Emily Brontë's case made it imperative that whoever undertook this belated introduction should show rather more than a perfunctory enthusiasm. Her alien and lonely state should have moved Mr. Clement Shorter to a passionate chivalry. It has not even moved him to revise his proofs with perfect piety. Perfect piety would have saved him from the oversight, innocent but deplorable, of attributing to Emily Brontë four poems which Emily Brontë could not possibly have written, which were in fact written by Anne: "Despondency", "In Memory of a Happy Day in February", "A Prayer", and "Confidence."[A] No doubt Mr. Shorter found them in Emily's handwriting; but how could he, how *could* he mistake Anne's voice for Emily's?

[Footnote A: Published among Charlotte Brontë's posthumous "Selections" in 1850.]

> My God (oh let me call Thee mine,
> Weak, wretched sinner though I be),
> My trembling soul would fain be Thine;
> My feeble faith still clings to Thee.

It is Anne's voice at her feeblest and most depressed.

It is, perhaps, a little ungrateful and ungracious to say these things, when but for Mr. Shorter we should not have had Emily's complete poems at all. And to accuse Mr. Shorter of present indifference (in the face of his previous achievements) would be iniquitous if it were not absurd; it would be biting the hand that feeds you. The pity is that, owing to a mere momentary lapse in him of the religious spirit, Mr. Shorter has missed his own opportunity. He does not seem to have quite realized the splendour of his "find". Nor has Sir William Robertson Nicoll seen fit to help him here. Sir William Robertson Nicoll deprecates any over-valuation of Mr. Clement Shorter's collection. "It is not claimed," he says, "for a moment that the intrinsic merits of the verses are of a special kind." And Mr. Clement Shorter is not much bolder in proffering his treasures. "No one can deny to them," he says, "a certain bibliographical interest."

Mr. Shorter is too modest. His collection includes one of the profoundest and most beautiful poems Emily Brontë ever wrote,[A] and at least one splendid ballad, "Douglas Ride".[B] Here is the ballad, or enough of it to show how live it is with sound and vision and speed. It was written by a girl of twenty:

> What rider up Gobeloin's glen
>   Has spurred his straining steed,
> And fast and far from living men
>   Has passed with maddening speed?
>
> I saw his hoof-prints mark the rock,
>   When swift he left the plain;
> I heard deep down the echoing shock
>   Re-echo back again.

* * * * *

> With streaming hair, and forehead bare,
>   And mantle waving wide,
> His master rides; the eagle there
>   Soars up on every side.
>
> The goats fly by with timid cry,
>   Their realm rashly won;
> They pause—he still ascends on high—
>   They gaze, but he is gone.

THE THREE BRONTËS

O gallant horse, hold on thy course;
  The road is tracked behind.
Spur, rider, spur, or vain thy force—
  Death comes on every wind.

* * * * *

Hark! through the pass with threatening crash
  Comes on the increasing roar!
But what shall brave the deep, deep wave,
  The deadly pass before?

Their feet are dyed in a darker tide,
  Who dare those dangers drear.
Their breasts have burst through the battle's worst,
  And why should they tremble here?

* * * * *

"Now, my brave men, this one pass more,
  This narrow chasm of stone,
And Douglas for our sovereign's gore
  Shall yield us back his own."

I hear their ever-rising tread
  Sound through the granite glen;
There is a tall pine overhead
  Held by the mountain men.

That dizzy bridge which no horse could track
  Has checked the outlaw's way;

> There like a wild beast turns he back,
>   And grimly stands at bay.
>
> Why smiles he so, when far below
>   He spies the toiling chase?
> The pond'rous tree swings heavily,
>   And totters from its place.
>
> They raise their eyes, for the sunny skies
>   Are lost in sudden shade:
> But Douglas neither shrinks nor flies,
>   He need not fear the dead.

[Footnote A: See pp. 207, 208.]

[Footnote B: I have removed the title from the preceding fragment to the ballad to which it obviously belongs.]

That is sufficiently unlike the Emily Brontë whom Charlotte edited. And there is one other poem that stands alone among her poems with a strange exotic beauty, a music, a rhythm and a magic utterly unlike any of the forms we recognize as hers:

> Gods of the old mythology
>   Arise in gloom and storm;
> Adramalec, bow down thy head,
>   Reveal, dark fiend, thy form.
> The giant sons of Anakim
>   Bowed lowest at thy shrine,
> And thy temple rose in Argola,
>   With its hallowed groves of vine;
> And there was eastern incense burnt,
>   And there were garments spread,
> With the fine gold decked and broidered,
>   And tinged with radiant red,

> With the radiant red of furnace flames
> That through the shadows shone
> As the full moon when on Sinai's top
> Her rising light is thrown.

It is undated and unsigned, and so unlike Emily Brontë that I should not be surprised if somebody were to rise up and prove that it is Coleridge or somebody. Heaven forbid that this blow should fall on Mr. Clement Shorter, and Sir William Robertson Nicoll, and on me. There is at least one reassuring line. "Reveal, dark fiend, thy form", has a decided ring of the Brontësque.

And here again, on many an otherwise negligible poem she has set her seal, she has scattered her fine things; thus:

> No; though the soil be wet with tears,
>   How fair so'er it grew,
> The vital sap once perished
>   Will never flow again;
> *And surer than that dwelling dread,*
> *The narrow dungeon of the dead,*
>   *Time parts the hearts of men.*

And again, she gives a vivid picture of war in four lines:

> In plundered churches piled with dead
>   The heavy charger neighed for food,
> The wounded soldier laid his head
>   'Neath roofless chambers splashed with blood.

Again, she has a vision:

> In all the hours of gloom
>   My soul was rapt away.
> I stood by a marble tomb
>   Where royal corpses lay.

A frightful thing appears to her, "a shadowy thing, most dim":

> And still it bent above,
> Its features still in view;
> *It seemed close by; and yet more far*
> *Than this world from the farthest star*
> *That tracks the boundless blue.*
>
> Indeed 'twas not the space
> Of earth or time between,
> But the sea of deep eternity,
> The gulf o'er which mortality
> Has never, never been.

The date is June 1837, a year earlier than the ballad. And here is the first sketch or germ of "The Old Stoic":

> Give we the hills our equal prayer,
>   Earth's breezy hills and heaven's blue sea,
> *I ask for nothing further here*
> *Than my own heart and liberty.*

And here is another poem, of a sterner and a sadder stoicism:

> There was a time when my cheek burned
>   To give such scornful words the lie,
> Ungoverned nature madly spurned
>   The law that bade it not defy.
> Oh, in the days of ardent youth
> I would have given my life for truth.
>
> For truth, for right, for liberty,
>   I would have gladly, freely died;
> And now I calmly bear and see
>   The vain man smile, the fool deride,

Though not because my heart is tame,
Though not for fear, though not for shame.

My soul still chokes at every tone
  Of selfish and self-clouded error;
My breast still braves the world alone,
  Steeled as it ever was to terror.
Only I know, howe'er I frown,
The same world will go rolling on.

October 1839. It is the worldly wisdom of twenty-one!

* * * * *

If this, the ballad and the rest, were all, the world would still be richer, by a wholly new conception of Emily Brontë, of her resources and her range.

But it is by no means all. And here we come to the opportunity which, owing to that temporary decline of fervour, Mr. Shorter has so unfortunately missed.

He might have picked out of the mass wherein they lie scattered, all but lost, sometimes barely recognizable, the fragments of a Titanic epic. He might have done something to build up again the fabric of that marvellous romance, that continuous dream, that stupendous and gorgeous fantasy in which Emily Brontë, for at least eleven years, lived and moved and had her being.

Until the publication of the unknown poems, it was possible to ignore the "Gondal Chronicles". They are not included in Mr. Clement Shorter's exhaustive list of early and unpublished manuscripts. Nobody knew anything about them except that they were part of a mysterious game of make-believe which Emily and the ever-innocent Anne played together, long after the age when most of us have given up make-believing. There are several references to the Chronicles in the diaries of Emily and Anne. Emily writes in 1841: "The Gondaland are at present in a threatening state, but there is no open rupture as yet. All the princes and princesses of the Royalty are at the Palace of Instruction." Anne wonders "whether the Gondaland will still be flourishing" in 1845. In 1845 Emily and Anne go for their first long journey together. "And during our excursion we were Ronald Macalgin, Henry Angora, Juliet Angusteena, Rosabella Esmaldan, Ella and Julian Egremont, Catharine Navarre, and Cordelia Fitzaphnold, escaping from the palaces of instruction to join the Royalists, who are hard pressed at present by the victorious Republicans. "The Gondals," Emily says, "still flourish bright as ever." Anne is not so sure. "We have not yet finished our 'Gondal Chronicles' that we began three years and a half ago. When will they be done? The Gondals are at present in a sad state. The Republicans are uppermost, but the Royalists are not quite overcome. The young sovereigns, with their brothers and sisters, are still at the Palace of Instruction. The Unique Society, about half a year ago, were wrecked on a desert island as they were returning from Gaul. They are still there, but we have not played at them much yet."

But there are no recognizable references to the Gondal poems. It is not certain whether Charlotte Brontë knew of their existence, not absolutely certain that Anne, who collaborated on the Gondals, knew.

"Brontë specialists" are agreed in dismissing the Chronicles as puerile. But the poems cannot be so dismissed. Written in lyric or ballad form, fluent at their worst and loose, but never feeble; powerful, vehement, and overflowing at their best, their cycle contains some of Emily Brontë's very finest verse. They are obscure, incoherent sometimes, because they are fragmentary; even poems apparently complete in themselves are fragments, scenes torn out of the vast and complicated epic drama. We have no clue to the history of the Gondals, whereby we can arrange these scenes in their right order. But dark and broken as they are, they yet trail an epic splendour, they bear the whole phantasmagoria of ancestral and of racial memories, of "old, unhappy, far-off things, and battles long ago". These songs and ballads, strung on no discernible thread, are the voice of an enchanted spirit, recalling the long roll of its secular existences; in whom nothing lives but that mysterious, resurgent memory.

The forms that move through these battles are obscure. You can pick out many of the Gondal poems by the recurring names of heroes and of lands. But where there are no names of heroes and of lands to guide you it is not easy to say exactly which poems are Gondal poems and which are not. But after careful examination and comparison you can make out at least eighty-three of them that are unmistakable, and ten doubtful.

All the battle-pieces and songs of battle, the songs of mourning and captivity and exile, the songs of heroism, martyrdom, defiance, songs, or fragments of songs, of magic and divination, and many of the love songs, belong to this cycle. What is more, many of the poems of eighteen-forty-six and of eighteen-fifty are Gondal poems.

For in the Gondal legend the idea of the Doomed Child, an idea that haunted Emily Brontë, recurs perpetually, and suggests that the Gondal legend is the proper place of "The Two Children", and "The Wanderer from the Fold", which appear in the posthumous Selections of eighteen-fifty. It certainly includes three at the very least of the poems of eighteen-forty-six: "The Outcast Mother", "A Death-Scene", and "Honour's Martyr".

It does not look, I own, as if this hunt for Gondal literature could interest a single human being; which is why nobody, so far as I know, has pursued it. And the placing of those four poems in the obscure Gondal legend would have nothing but "a bibliographical interest" were it not that, when placed there, they show at once the main track of the legend. And the main track of the legend brings you straight to the courses of *Wuthering Heights* and of the love poems.

The sources of *Wuthering Heights* have been the dream and the despair of the explorer, long before Mrs. Humphry Ward tried to find them in the *Tales of Hoffmann*. And "Remembrance", one of the most passionate love poems in the language, stood alone and apart from every other thing that Emily Brontë had written. It was awful and mysterious in its loneliness.

But I believe that "Remembrance" also may be placed in the Gondal legend without any violence to its mystery.

For supreme in the Gondal legend is the idea of a mighty and disastrous passion, a woman's passion for the defeated, the dishonoured, and the outlawed lover; a creature superb in evil, like Heathcliff, and like Heathcliff tragic and unspeakably mournful in his doom. He or some hero like him is "Honour's Martyr".

> To-morrow, Scorn will blight my name,
>   And Hate will trample me,
> Will load me with a coward's shame—
>   A traitor's perjury.
>
> False friends will launch their covert sneers
>   True friends will wish me dead;
> And I shall cause the bitterest tears
>   That you have ever shed.

Like Heathcliff, he is the "unblessed, unfriended child"; the child of the Outcast Mother, abandoned on the moor.

> Forests of heather, dark and long,
>   Wave their brown branching arms above;
> And they must soothe thee with their song,
>   And they must shield my child of love.

* * * * *

> Wakes up the storm more madly wild,
>   The mountain drifts are tossed on high;
> Farewell, unblessed, unfriended child,
>   I cannot bear to watch thee die.

In an unmistakable Gondal song Geraldine's lover calls her to the tryst on the moor. In the Gondal poem "Geraldine", she has her child with her in a woodland cavern, and she prays over it wildly:

> "Bless it! My Gracious God!" I cried,
>   "Preserve Thy mortal shrine,
> For Thine own sake, be Thou its guide,
>   And keep it still divine—
>
> "Say, sin shall never blanch that cheek,
>   Nor suffering change that brow.
> Speak, in Thy mercy, Maker, speak,
>   And seal it safe from woe."

* * * * *

> The revellers in the city slept,
>   My lady in her woodland bed;
> I watching o'er her slumber wept,
>   As one who mourns the dead.

Geraldine therefore is the Outcast Mother. In "The Two Children" the doom gathers round the child.

> Heavy hangs the raindrop
>   From the burdened spray;

THE THREE BRONTËS

Heavy broods the damp mist
  On uplands far away.

Heavy looms the dull sky,
  Heavy rolls the sea;
And heavy throbs the young heart
  Beneath that lonely tree.

Never has a blue streak
  Cleft the clouds since morn
Never has his grim fate
  Smiled since he was born.

Frowning on the infant,
  Shadowing childhood's joy.
Guardian-angel knows not
  That melancholy boy.

* * * * *

Blossom—that the west wind
  Has never wooed to blow,
Scentless are thy petals,
  Thy dew is cold as snow!

Soul—where kindred kindness
  No early promise woke,
Barren is thy beauty,
  As weed upon a rock.

Wither—soul and blossom!
  You both were vainly given:

Earth reserves no blessing
For the unblest of Heaven.

The doomed child of the outcast mother is the doomed man, and, by the doom, himself an outcast. The other child, the "Child of delight, with sun-bright hair", has vowed herself to be his guardian angel. Their drama is obscure; but you make out that it is the doomed child, and not Branwell Brontë, who is "The Wanderer from the Fold".

How few, of all the hearts that loved,
  Are grieving for thee now;
And why should mine to-night be moved
  With such a sense of woe?

Too often thus, when left alone,
  Where none my thoughts can see,
Comes back a word, a passing tone
  From thy strange history.

* * * * *

An anxious gazer from the shore—
  I marked the whitening wave,
And wept above thy fate the more
  Because—I could not save.

It recks not now, when all is over;
  But yet my heart will be
A mourner still, though friend and lover
  Have both forgotten thee.

Compare with this that stern elegy in Mr. Shorter's collection,

"Shed no tears o'er that tomb." A recent critic has referred this poem of reprobation also to Branwell Brontë—as if Emily could possibly have written like this of Branwell:

> Shed no tears o'er that tomb,
>   For there are angels weeping;
> Mourn not him whose doom
>   Heaven itself is mourning.

* * * * *

> ... he who slumbers there
>   His bark will strive no more
> Across the waters of despair
>   To reach that glorious shore.
>
> The time of grace is past,
>   And mercy, scorned and tried,
> Forsakes to utter wrath at last
>   The soul so steeled by pride.
>
> That wrath will never spare,
>   Will never pity know;
> Will mock its victim's maddened prayer,
>   With triumph in his woe.
>
> Shut from his Maker's smile
>   The accursed man shall be;
> For mercy reigns a little while,
>   But hate eternally.

This is obviously related to "The Two Children", and that again to "The Wanderer from the Fold". Obviously, too, the woman's lament in "The Wanderer from the Fold" recalls the Gondal woman's lament for her dishonoured lover. For there are two voices that speak and answer each other, the voice of reprobation, and the voice of passion and pity. This is the "Gondal Woman's Lament":

> Far, far is mirth withdrawn:
> 'Tis three long hours before the morn,
> And I watch lonely, drearily;
> So come, thou shade, commune with me.
>
> Deserted one! thy corpse lies cold,
> And mingled with a foreign mould.
> Year after year the grass grows green
> Above the dust where thou hast been.
>
> I will not name thy blighted name,
> Tarnished by unforgotten shame,
> Though not because my bosom torn
> Joins the mad world in all its scorn.
>
> Thy phantom face is dark with woe,
> Tears have left ghastly traces there,
> Those ceaseless tears! I wish their flow
> Could quench thy wild despair.
>
> They deluge my heart like the rain
> On cursed Zamorna's howling plain.
> Yet when I hear thy foes deride,
> I must cling closely to thy side.
>
> Our mutual foes! They will not rest
> From trampling on thy buried breast.
> Glutting their hatred with the doom
> They picture thine beyond the tomb.

(Which is what they did in the song of reprobation. But passion and pity know better. They know that)

> ... God is not like human kind,
> Man cannot read the Almighty mind;
> Vengeance will never torture thee,
> Nor hurt thy soul eternally.

* * * * *

> What have I dreamt? He lies asleep,
> With whom my heart would vainly weep;
> *He* rests, and *I* endure the woe
> That left his spirit long ago.

This poem is not quoted for its beauty or its technique, but for its important place in the story. You can track the great Gondal hero down by that one fantastic name, "Zamorna". You have thus four poems, obviously related; and a fifth that links them, obviously, with the Gondal legend.

It is difficult to pick out from the confusion of these unsorted fragments all the heroes of Emily Brontë's saga. There is Gleneden, who kills a tyrant and is put in prison for it. There is Julius Angora, who "lifts his impious eye" in the cathedral where the monarchs of Gondal are gathered; who leads the patriots of Gondal to the battle of Almedore, and was defeated there, and fell with his mortal enemy. He is beloved of Rosina, a crude prototype of Catherine Earnshaw. "King Julius left the south country" and remained in danger in the northern land because a passion for Rosina kept him there. There is also Douglas of the "Ride". He appears again in the saga of the Queen Augusta, the woman of the "brown mountain side". But who he was, and what he was doing, and whether he killed Augusta or somebody else killed her, I cannot for the life of me make out. Queen Augusta, like Catherine Earnshaw, is a creature of passion and jealousy, and her lover had been faithless. She sings that savage song of defiance and hatred and lamentation: "Light up thy halls!"

> Oh! could I see thy lids weighed down in cheerless woe;
> Too full to hide their tears, too stern to overflow;
> Oh! could I know thy soul with equal grief was torn,
> This fate might be endured—this anguish might be borne.
>
> How gloomy grows the night! 'Tis Gondal's wind that blows;
> I shall not tread again the deep glens where it rose,
> I feel it on my face——Where, wild blast! dost thou roam?
> What do we, wanderer! here, so far away from home?
>
> I do not need thy breath to cool my death-cold brow;
> But go to that far land where she is shining now;
> Tell her my latest wish, tell her my dreary doom;
> Say that my pangs are past, but *hers* are yet to come.

And there is Fernando, who stole his love from Zamorna. He is a sort of shadowy forerunner of Edgar Linton.

There is the yeoman Percy, the father of Mary whom Zamorna loved. And there is Zamorna.

A large group of poems in the legend refer, obviously, I think, to the same person. Zamorna is the supreme hero, the Achilles of this northern Iliad. He is the man of sin, the "son of war and love", the child "unblessed of heaven", abandoned by its mother, cradled in the heather and rocked by the winter storm, the doomed child, grown to its doom, like Heathcliff. His story is obscure and broken, but when all the Zamorna poems are sorted from the rest, you make out that, like Heathcliff, he ravished from her home the daughter of his mortal enemy (with the difference that Zamorna loves Mary); and that like Heathcliff he was robbed of the woman that he loved. The passions of Zamorna are the passions of Heathcliff. He dominates a world of savage loves and mortal enmities like the world of *Wuthering Heights*. There are passages in this saga that reveal the very aspect of the soul of Heathcliff. Here are some of them.

Zamorna, in prison, cries out to his "false friend and treacherous guide":

> "If I have sinned; long, long ago
> That sin was purified by woe.
> I have suffered on through night and day,
> I've trod a dark and frightful way."

It is what Heathcliff says to Catherine Earnshaw: "I've fought through a bitter life since I last heard your voice."

And again:

> If grief for grief can touch thee,
>   If answering woe for woe,
> If any ruth can melt thee,
>   Come to me now.

It is the very voice of Heathcliff calling to Cathy.

Again, he is calling to "Percy", the father of Mary, his bride, the rose that he plucked from its parent stem, that died from the plucking.

> Bitterly, deeply I've drunk of thy woe;
> When thy stream was troubled, did mine calmly flow?
> And yet I repent not; I'd crush thee again
> If our vessels sailed adverse on life's stormy main.
> But listen! The earth is our campaign of war,

THE THREE BRONTËS

* * * * *

Is there not havoc and carnage for thee
Unless thou couchest thy lance at me?

He proposes to unite their arms.

Then might thy Mary bloom blissfully still
This hand should ne'er work her sorrow or ill.

* * * * *

What! shall Zamorna go down to the dead
With blood on his hands that he wept to have shed?

The alliance is refused. Percy is crushed. Mary is dying, the rose is withering.

Its faded buds already lie
To deck my coffin when I die.
Bring them here—'twill not be long,
'Tis the last word of the woeful song;
And the final and dying words are sung
To the discord of lute strings all unstrung.

* * * * *

Have I crushed you, Percy? I'd raise once more
The beacon-light on the rocky shore.
Percy, my love is so true and deep,

That though kingdoms should wail and worlds should weep,
  I'd fling the brand in the hissing sea,
  The brand that must burn unquenchably.
Your rose is mine; when the sweet leaves fade,
They must be the chaplet to wreathe my head
The blossoms to deck my home with the dead.

Zamorna is tenderer than Heathcliff. He laments for his rose.

On its bending stalk a bonny flower
  In a yeoman's home close grew;
It had gathered beauty from sunshine and shower,
  From moonlight and silent dew.

* * * * *

Keenly his flower the yeoman guarded,
  He watched it grow both day and night;
From the frost, from the wind, from the storm he warded
  That flush of roseate light.
And ever it glistened bonnilie
Under the shade of the old yew-tree.

* * * * *

The rose is blasted, withered, blighted
  Its root has felt a worm,
And like a heart beloved and slighted,
  Failed, faded, shrunk its form.

THE THREE BRONTËS

> Bud of beauty, bonny flower,
>   I stole thee from thy natal bower.

I was the worm that withered thee....
And he sings of Mary, on her death-bed in her delirium. He will not believe that she is dying.

> Oh! say not that her vivid dreams
>   Are but the shattered glass
> Which but because more broken, gleams
>   More brightly in the grass.
> Her spirit is the unfathomed lake
> Whose face the sudden tempests break
>   To one tormented roar;
> But as the wild winds sink in peace
> All those disturbed waves decrease
> Till each far-down reflection is
>   As life-like as before.

Her death is not the worst.

> I cannot weep as once I wept
>   Over my western beauty's grave.

* * * * *

> I am speaking of a later stroke,
>   A death the dream of yesterday,
> Still thinking of my latest shock,
>   A noble friendship torn away.
> I feel and say that I am cast
>   From hope, and peace, and power, and pride

* * * * *

> Without a voice to speak to you
>   Save that deep gong which tolled my doom,
> And made my dread iniquity
>   Look darker than my deepest gloom.

But the crucial passage (for the sources) is the scene in the yeoman's hall where Zamorna comes to Percy. He comes stealthily.

> That step he might have used before
> When stealing on to lady's bower,
> Forth at the same still twilight hour,
> For the moon now bending mild above
> Showed him a son of war and love.
> His eye was full of that sinful fire
> Which oft unhallowed passions light.
> It spoke of quickly kindled ire,
> Of love too warm, and wild, and bright.
> Bright, but yet sullied, love that could never
> Bring good in rising, leave peace in decline,
> Woe to the gifted, crime to the giver....

* * * * *

> Now from his curled and shining hair,
> Circling the brow of marble fair,
> His dark, keen eyes on Percy gaze
> With stern and yet repenting rays.

THE THREE BRONTËS

* * * * *

He loves Percy whose rose was his, and he hates him, as Heathcliff might have loved and hated, but with less brutality.

> Young savage! how he bends above
> The object of his wrath and love,
> How tenderly his fingers press
> The hand that shrinks from their caress.

The yeoman turns on "the man of sin".
What brought you here? I called you not

* * * * *

> Are you a hawk to follow the prey,
> When mangled it flutters feebly away?
> A sleuth-hound to track the deer by his blood,
> When wounded he wins to the darkest wood,
> There, if he can, to die alone?

It might have been Heathcliff and a Linton.
So much for Zamorna.
Finally, there are two poems in Mr. Shorter's collection that, verse for prose, might have come straight out of *Wuthering Heights*. One (inspired by Byron) certainly belongs to the Zamorna legend of the Gondal cycle.

> And now the house-dog stretched once more
> His limbs upon the glowing floor;
> The children half resume their play,
> Though from the warm hearth scared away;
> The good-wife left her spinning-wheel
> And spread with smiles the evening meal;

> The shepherd placed a seat and pressed
> To their poor fare the unknown guest,
> And he unclasped his mantle now,
> And raised the covering from his brow,
> Said, voyagers by land and sea
> Were seldom feasted daintily,
> And cheered his host by adding stern
> He'd no refinement to unlearn.

Which is what Heathcliff would have said sternly. Observe the effect of him.

> A silence settled on the room,
> The cheerful welcome sank to gloom;
> But not those words, though cold or high,
> So froze their hospitable joy.
> No—there was something in his face,
> Some nameless thing which hid not grace,
> And something in his voice's tone
> Which turned their blood as chill as stone.
> The ringlets of his long black hair
> Fell o'er a cheek most ghastly fair.
> Youthful he seemed—but worn as they
> Who spend too soon their youthful day.
> When his glance dropped, 'twas hard to quell
> Unbidden feelings' hidden swell;
> And Pity scarce her tears could hide,
> So sweet that brow with all its pride.
> But when upraised his eye would dart
> An icy shudder through the heart,
> Compassion changed to horror then,
> And fear to meet that gaze again.
>
> It was not hatred's tiger-glare,
> Nor the wild anguish of despair;

> It was not either misery
> Which quickens friendship's sympathy;
> No—lightning all unearthly shone
> Deep in that dark eye's circling zone,
> Such withering lightning as we deem
> None but a spirit's look may beam;
> And glad were all when he turned away
> And wrapt him in his mantle grey,
> And hid his head upon his arm,
> And veiled from view his basilisk charm.

That, I take it, is Zamorna, that Byronic hero, again; but it is also uncommonly like Heathcliff, with "his basilisk eyes". And it is dated July 1839, seven years before *Wuthering Heights* was written.

The other crucial instance is a nameless poem to the Earth.

> I see around me piteous tombstones grey
> Stretching their shadows far away.
> Beneath the turf my footsteps tread
> Lie low and lone the silent dead;
> Beneath the turf, beneath the mould,
> For ever dark, for ever cold.
> And my eyes cannot hold the tears
> That memory hoards from vanished years.
> For Time and Death and mortal pain
> Give wounds that will not heal again.
> Let me remember half the woe
> I've seen and heard and felt below,
> And heaven itself, so pure and blest,
> Could never give my spirit rest.
> Sweet land of light! Thy children fair
> Know nought akin to our despair;
> Nor have they felt, nor can they tell
> What tenants haunt each mortal cell,

What gloomy guests we hold within,
Torments and madness, fear and sin!
Well, may they live in ecstasy
Their long eternity of joy;
At least we would not bring them down
With us to weep, with us to groan.
No, Earth would wish no other sphere
To taste her cup of suffering drear;
She turns from heaven a tearless eye
And only mourns that *we* must die!
Ah mother! what shall comfort thee
In all this boundless misery?
To cheer our eager eyes awhile,
We see thee smile, how fondly smile!
But who reads not through the tender glow
Thy deep, unutterable woe?
Indeed no darling hand above
Can cheat thee of thy children's love.
We all, in life's departing shine,
Our last dear longings blend with thine,
And struggle still, and strive to trace
With clouded gaze thy darling face.
We would not leave our nature home
For *any* world beyond the tomb.
No, mother, on thy kindly breast
Let us be laid in lasting rest,
Or waken but to share with thee
A mutual immortality.

There is the whole spirit of *Wuthering Heights*; the spirit of Catherine Earnshaw's dream; the spirit that in the last page broods over the moorland graveyard. It is instinct with a more than pagan adoration of the tragic earth, adored because of her tragedy.

It would be dangerous to assert positively that "Remembrance" belongs to the same song-cycle; but it undoubtedly belongs to the same cycle, or rather cyclone, of passion; the cyclone that rages in the hearts of Heathcliff and of Catherine. The genius of Emily Brontë was so far dramatic that, if you could divide her poems into the personal and impersonal, the impersonal would be found in a mass out of all proportion to the other. But, with very few exceptions, you cannot so divide them; for in her continuous and sustaining dream, the vision that lasted for at least eleven years of her life, from eighteen-thirty-four, the earliest date of any known Gondal poem, to eighteen-forty-five, the last appearance of the legend, she *was* these people; she lived, indistinguishably and interchangeably, their tumultuous and passionate life. Sometimes she is the lonely spirit that looks on in immortal irony, raised above good and evil. More often she is a happy god, immanent in his restless and manifold creations, rejoicing in this multiplication of himself. It is she who fights and rides, who loves and hates, and suffers and defies. She heads one poem naïvely: "To the Horse Black Eagle that I rode at the Battle of Zamorna." The horse *I* rode! If it were not glorious, it would be (when you think what her life was in that Parsonage) most mortally pathetic.

But it is all in keeping. For, as she could dare the heavenly, divine adventure, so there was no wild and ardent adventure of the earth she did not claim.

* * * * *

Love of life and passionate adoration of the earth, adoration and passion fiercer than any pagan knew, burns in *Wuthering Heights*. And if that were all, it would be impossible to say whether her mysticism or her paganism most revealed the soul of Emily Brontë.

In *Wuthering Heights* we are plunged apparently into a world of most unspiritual lusts and hates and cruelties; into the very darkness and thickness of elemental matter; a world that would be chaos, but for the iron Necessity that brings its own terrible order, its own implacable law of lust upon lust begotten, hate upon hate, and cruelty upon cruelty, through the generations of Heathcliffs and of Earnshaws.

Hindley Earnshaw is brutal to the foundling, Heathcliff, and degrades him. Heathcliff, when his hour comes, pays back his wrong with the interest due. He is brutal beyond brutality to Hindley Earnshaw, and he degrades Hareton, Hindley's son, as he himself was degraded; but he is not brutal to him. The frustrated passion of Catherine Earnshaw for Heathcliff, and of Heathcliff for Catherine, hardly knows itself from hate; they pay each other back torture for torture, and pang for hopeless pang. When Catherine marries Edgar Linton, Heathcliff marries Isabella, Edgar's sister, in order that he may torture to perfection Catherine and Edgar and Isabella. His justice is more than poetic. The love of Catherine Earnshaw was all that he possessed. He knows that he has lost it through the degradation that he owes to Hindley Earnshaw. It is because an Earnshaw and a Linton between them have robbed him of all that he possessed, that, when his hour comes, he pays himself back by robbing the Lintons and the Earnshaws of all that *they* possess, their Thrushcross Grange and Wuthering Heights. He loathes above all loathely creatures, Linton, his own son by Isabella. The white-blooded thing is so sickly that he can hardly keep it alive. But with an unearthly cruelty he cherishes, he nourishes this spawn till he can marry it on its death-bed to the younger Catherine, the child of Catherine Earnshaw and of Edgar Linton. This supreme deed accomplished, he lets the creature die, so that Thrushcross Grange may fall into his hands. Judged by his bare deeds, Heathcliff seems a monster of evil, a devil without any fiery infernal splendour, a mean and sordid devil.

But—and this is what makes Emily Brontë's work stupendous—not for a moment can you judge Heathcliff by his bare deeds. Properly speaking, there are no bare deeds to judge him by. Each deed comes wrapt in its own infernal glamour, trailing a cloud of supernatural splendour. The whole drama moves on a plane of reality superior to any deed. The spirit of it, like Emily Brontë's spirit, is superbly regardless of the material event. As far as material action goes Heathcliff is singularly inert. He never seems to raise a hand to help his vengeance. He lets things take their course. He lets Catherine marry Edgar Linton and remain married to him. He lets Isabella's passion satisfy itself. He lets Hindley Earnshaw drink himself to death. He lets Hareton sink to the level of a boor. He lets Linton die. His most overt and violent action is the capture of the younger Catherine. And even there he takes advantage of the accident that brings her to the door of Wuthering Heights. He watches and bides his time with the intentness of a brooding spirit that in all material happenings seeks its own. He makes them his instruments of vengeance. And Heathcliff's vengeance, like his passion for Catherine, is an immortal and immaterial thing. He shows how little he thinks of sordid, tangible possession; for, when his vengeance is complete, when Edgar Linton and Linton Heathcliff are dead and their lands and houses are his, he becomes utterly indifferent. He falls into a melancholy. He neither eats nor drinks. He shuts himself up in Cathy's little room and is found dead there, lying on Cathy's bed.

If there never was anything less heavenly, less Christian, than this drama, there never was anything less earthly, less pagan. There is no name for it. It is above all our consecrated labels and distinctions. It has been called a Greek tragedy, with the Aeschylean motto, [Greek: to drasanti pathein]. But it is not Greek any more than it is Christian; and if it has a moral, its moral is far more [Greek: to pathonti pathein]. It is the drama of suffering born of suffering, and confined strictly within the boundaries of the soul.

Madame Duclaux (whose criticism of *Wuthering Heights* is not to be surpassed or otherwise gainsaid) finds in it a tragedy of inherited evil. She thinks that Emily Brontë was greatly swayed by the doctrine of heredity. "'No use,' she seems to be saying, 'in waiting for the children of evil parents to grow, of their own will and unassisted, straight and noble. The very quality of their will is as inherited as their eyes and hair. Heathcliff is no fiend or goblin; the untrained, doomed child of some half-savage sailor's holiday, violent and treacherous. And how far shall we hold the sinner responsible for a nature which is itself the punishment of some forefather's crime?'"

All this, I cannot help thinking, is alien to the spirit of *Wuthering Heights*, and to its greatness. It is not really any problem of heredity that we have here. Heredity is, in fact, ignored. Heathcliff's race and parentage are unknown. There is no resemblance between the good old Earnshaws, who adopted him, and their son Hindley. Hareton does not inherit Hindley's drunkenness or his cruelty. It is not through any physical consequence of his father's vices that Hareton suffers. Linton is in no physical sense the son of Heathcliff. If Catherine Linton inherits something of Catherine Earnshaw's charm and temper, it is because the younger Catherine belongs to another world; she is an inferior and more physical creature. She has nothing in her of Catherine Earnshaw's mutinous passion, the immortal and unearthly passion which made that Catherine alive and killed her. Catherine Linton's "little romance" is altogether another affair.

The world of Heathcliff and Catherine Earnshaw is a world of spiritual affinities, of spiritual contacts and recoils where love begets and bears love, and hate is begotten of hate and born of shame. Even Linton Heathcliff, that "whey-faced, whining wretch", that physical degenerate, demonstrates the higher law. His weakness is begotten by his father's loathing on his mother's terror.

Never was a book written with a more sublime ignoring of the physical. You only get a taste of it once in Isabella's unwholesome love for Heathcliff; that is not passion, it is sentiment, and it is thoroughly impure. And you get a far-off vision of it again in Isabella's fear of Heathcliff. Heathcliff understood her. He says of her, "'No brutality disgusted her.... I've sometimes relented, from pure lack of invention, in my experiments on what she could endure and still creep shamefully back.'" This civilized creature is nearer to the animals, there is more of the earth in her than in Catherine or in Heathcliff. They are elemental beings, if you like, but their element is fire. They are clean, as all fiery, elemental things are clean.

True, their love found violent physical expression; so that M. Maeterlinck can say of them and their creator: "We feel that one must have lived for thirty years under chains of burning kisses to learn what she has learned; to dare so confidently set forth, with such minuteness, such unerring certainty, the delirium of those two lovers of *Wuthering Heights*; to mark the self-conflicting movements of the tenderness that would make suffer, and the cruelty that would make glad, the felicity that prayed for death, and the despair that clung to life, the repulsion that desired, the desire drunk with repulsion—love surcharged with hatred, hatred staggering beneath its load of love."[A]

[Footnote A: *Wisdom and Destiny*, translated by Alfred Sutro.]

True; but the passion that consumes Catherine and Heathcliff, that burns their bodies and destroys them, is nine-tenths a passion of the soul. It taught them nothing of the sad secrets of the body. Thus Catherine's treachery to Heathcliff is an unconscious treachery. It is her innocence that makes it possible. She goes to Edgar Linton's arms with blind eyes, in utter, childlike ignorance, not knowing what she does till it is done and she is punished for it. She is punished for the sin of sins, the sundering of the body from the soul. All her life after she sees her sin. She has taken her body, torn it apart and given it to Edgar Linton, and Heathcliff has her soul.

"'You love Edgar Linton,' Nelly Dean says, 'and Edgar loves you ... where is the obstacle?'

"'*Here!* and *here!*' replied Catherine, striking one hand on her forehead, and the other on her breast: 'in whichever place the soul lives. In my soul and in my heart, I'm convinced I'm wrong.'... 'I've no more business to marry Edgar Linton than I have to be in heaven; and if the wicked man in there hadn't brought Heathcliff so low, I shouldn't have thought of it. It would degrade me to marry Heathcliff now; so he shall never know how I love him, and that, not because he's handsome, Nelly, but because he's more myself than I am. Whatever our souls are made of, his and mine are the same.'"

Not only are they made of the same stuff, but Heathcliff *is* her soul.

"'I cannot express it; but surely you and everybody have a notion that there is, or should be, an existence of yours beyond you. What were the use of my creation, if I were entirely contained here? My great miseries in this world have been Heathcliff's miseries ... my great thought in living is himself.... Nelly! I *am* Heathcliff! He's always, always in my mind: not as a pleasure, any more than I am a pleasure to myself, but as my own being.'"

That is her "secret".

Of course, there is Cathy's other secret—her dream, which passes for Emily Brontë's "pretty piece of Paganism". But it is only one side of Emily Brontë. And it is only one side of Catherine Earnshaw. When Heathcliff turns from her for a moment in that last scene of passion, she says: "'Oh, you see, Nelly, he would not relent a moment to keep me out of the grave. *That* is how I'm loved! Well, never mind. That is not *my* Heathcliff. I shall love mine yet; and take him with me: he's in my soul. And,' she added musingly, 'the thing that irks me most is this shattered prison, after all. I'm tired of being enclosed here. I'm wearying to escape into that glorious world, and to be always there: not seeing it dimly through tears, and yearning for it through the walls of an aching heart; but really with it and in it. Nelly, you think you are better and more fortunate than I; in full health and strength; you are sorry for me—very soon that will be altered. I shall be sorry for *you*. I shall be incomparably above and beyond you all.'"

True, adoration of Earth, the All-Mother, runs like a choric hymn through all the tragedy. Earth is the mother and the nurse of these children. They are brought to her for their last bed, and she gives them the final consolation.

Yet, after all, the end of this wild northern tragedy is far enough from Earth, the All-Mother. The tumult of *Wuthering Heights* ceases when Heathcliff sickens. It sinks suddenly into the peace and silence of exhaustion. And the drama closes, not in hopeless gloom, the agony of damned souls, but in redemption, reconciliation.

Catherine, the child of Catherine and of Edgar Linton, loves Hareton, the child of Hindley Earnshaw. The evil spirit that possessed these two dies with the death of Heathcliff. The younger Catherine is a mixed creature, half-spiritualized by much suffering. Hareton is a splendid animal, unspiritualized and unredeemed. Catherine redeems him; and you gather that by that act of redemption, somehow, the souls of Catherine and Heathcliff are appeased.

The whole tremendous art of the book is in this wringing of strange and terrible harmony out of raging discord. It ends on a sliding cadence, soft as a sigh of peace only just conscious after pain.

"I sought, and soon discovered, the three headstones on the slope next the moor: the middle one grey and half-buried in heath; Edgar Linton's only harmonized by the turf and moss creeping up its foot; Heathcliff's still bare.

"I lingered round them, under that benign sky: watched the moths fluttering among the heath and harebells, listened to the soft wind breathing through the grass, and wondered how anyone could ever imagine unquiet slumbers for the sleepers in that quiet earth."

* * * * *

But that is not the real end, any more than Lockwood's arrival at Wuthering Heights is the beginning. It is only Lockwood recovering himself; the natural man's drawing breath after the passing of the supernatural.

For it was not conceivable that the more than human love of Heathcliff and Catherine should cease with the dissolution of their bodies. It was not conceivable that Catherine, by merely dying in the fifteenth chapter, should pass out of the tale. As a matter of fact, she never does pass out of it. She is more in it than ever.

For the greater action of the tragedy is entirely on the invisible and immaterial plane; it is the pursuing, the hunting to death of an earthly creature by an unearthly passion. You are made aware of it at the very beginning when the ghost of the child Catherine is heard and felt by Lockwood; though it is Heathcliff that she haunts. It begins in the hour after Catherine's death, upon Heathcliff's passionate invocation: "'Catherine Earnshaw, may you not rest so long as I am living! You said I killed you—haunt me, then! The murdered *do* haunt their murderers, I believe. I know that ghosts *have* wandered on earth. Be with me always—take any form—drive me mad! Only *do* not leave me in this abyss, where I cannot find you! Oh God! it is unbearable! I *cannot* live without my life! I *cannot* live without my soul!'"

It begins and is continued through eighteen years. He cannot see her, but he is aware of her. He is first aware on the evening of the day she is buried. He goes to the graveyard and breaks open the new-made grave, saying to himself, "'I'll have her in my arms again! If she be cold, I'll think it is the north wind that chills *me*; and if she be motionless, it is sleep.'" A sighing, twice repeated, stops him. "'I appeared to feel the warm breath of it displacing the sleet-laden wind. I knew no living thing in flesh and blood was by; but as certainly as you perceive the approach to some substantial body in the dark, though it cannot be discerned, so certainly I felt Cathy was there; not under me, but on the earth.... Her presence was with me; it remained while I refilled the grave, and led me home.'"

But she cannot get through to him completely, because of the fleshly body that he wears.

He goes up to his room, his room and hers. "'I looked round impatiently—I felt her by me—I could *almost* see her, and yet I *could not!*... She showed herself, as she often was in life, a devil to me! And since then, sometimes more and sometimes less, I've been the sport of that intolerable torture!... When I sat in the house with Hareton, it seemed that on going out I should meet her; when I walked on the moors I should meet her coming in. When I went from home, I hastened to return; she *must* be somewhere at the Heights, I was certain! And when I slept in her chamber—I was beaten out of that. I couldn't lie there; for the moment I closed my eyes, she was either outside the window, or sliding back the panels, or entering the room, or even resting her darling head on the same pillow as she did when a child; and I must open my lids to see. And so I opened and closed them a hundred times a night—to be always disappointed! It racked me!... It was a strange way of killing: not by inches, but by fractions of hair-breadths, to beguile me with the spectre of a hope through eighteen years!'"

In all Catherine's appearances you feel the impulse towards satisfaction of a soul frustrated of its passion, avenging itself on the body that betrayed it. It has killed Catherine's body. It will kill Heathcliff's; for it *must* get through to him. And he knows it.

Heathcliff's brutalities, his cruelties, the long-drawn accomplishment of his revenge, are subordinate to this supreme inner drama, this wearing down of the flesh by the lust of a remorseless spirit.

Here are the last scenes of the final act. Heathcliff is failing. "'Nelly,' he says, 'there's a strange change approaching: I'm in its shadow at present. I take so little interest in my daily life, that I hardly remember to eat or drink. Those two who have left the room'" (Catherine Linton and Hareton) "'are the only objects which retain a distinct material appearance to me.... Five minutes ago, Hareton seemed a personification of my youth, not a human being: I felt to him in such a variety of ways that it would have been impossible to have accosted him rationally. In the first place, his startling likeness to Catherine connected him fearfully with her. That, however, which you may suppose the most potent to arrest my imagination, is actually the least: for what is not connected with her to me? and what does not recall her? I cannot look down to this floor, but her features are shaped in the flags? In every cloud, in every tree—filling the air at night, and caught by glimpses in every object by day—I am devoured with her image! The most ordinary faces of men and women—my own features—mock me with a resemblance. The entire world is a dreadful collection of memoranda that she did exist, and that I have lost her.'...

"'But what do you mean by a *change*, Mr. Heathcliff?' I said, alarmed at his manner....

"'I shall not know till it comes,' he said, 'I'm only half conscious of it now.'"

A few days pass. He grows more and more abstracted and detached. One morning Nelly Dean finds him downstairs, risen late.

"I put a basin of coffee before him. He drew it nearer, and then rested his arms on the table, and looked at the opposite wall, as I supposed, surveying one particular portion, up and down, with glittering, restless eyes, and with such eager interest that he stopped breathing during half a minute together....

"'Mr. Heathcliff! master!' I cried, 'don't, for God's sake stare as if you saw an unearthly vision.'

"'Don't, for God's sake, shout so loud,' he replied. 'Turn round, and tell me, are we by ourselves?'

"'Of course,' was my answer, 'of course we are.'

"Still, I involuntarily obeyed him, as if I were not quite sure. With a sweep of his hand he cleared a space in front of the breakfast-things, and leant forward more at his ease.

"Now I perceived that he was not looking at the wall; for,

when I regarded him alone, it seemed exactly that he gazed at something within two yards' distance. And, whatever it was, it communicated, apparently, both pleasure and pain in exquisite extremes: at least the anguished, yet raptured, expression of his countenance suggested that idea. The fancied object was not fixed: either his eyes pursued it with unwearied diligence, and, even in speaking to me, were never weaned away. I vainly reminded him of his protracted abstinence from food: if he stirred to touch anything in compliance with my entreaties, if he stretched his hand out to get a piece of bread, his fingers clenched before they reached it, and remained on the table, forgetful of their aim."

He cannot sleep; and at dawn of the next day he comes to the door of his room—Cathy's room—and calls Nelly to him. She remonstrates with him for his neglect of his body's health, and of his soul's.

"'Your cheeks are hollow, and your eyes bloodshot, like a person starving with hunger, and going blind with loss of sleep.'

"'It is not my fault that I cannot eat or rest,' he said.... 'I'll do both as soon as I possibly can ... as to repenting of my injustices, I've done no injustice, and I repent of nothing. I am too happy; and yet I'm not happy enough. My soul's bliss kills my body, but does not satisfy itself.'" ... "In the afternoon, while Joseph and Hareton were at their work, he came into the kitchen again, and, with a wild look, bid me come and sit in the house: he wanted somebody with him. I declined; telling him plainly that his strange talk and manner frightened me, and I had neither the nerve nor the will to be his companion alone.

"'I believe you think me a fiend,' he said, with his dismal laugh: 'something too horrible to live under a decent roof.' Then, turning to Catherine, who was there, and who drew behind me at his approach, he added, half sneeringly: 'Will *you* come, chuck? I'll not hurt you. No! to you I've made myself worse than the devil. Well, there is *one* who won't shrink from my company! By God! she's relentless. Oh, damn it! It's unutterably too much for flesh and blood to bear—even mine.'"

It is Heathcliff's susceptibility to this immaterial passion, the fury with which he at once sustains and is consumed by it, that makes him splendid.

Peace under green grass could never be the end of Heathcliff or of such a tragedy as *Wuthering Heights*. Its real end is the tale told by the shepherd whom Lockwood meets on the moor.

"'I was going to the Grange one evening—a dark evening, threatening thunder—and, just at the turn of the Heights, I encountered a little boy with a sheep and two lambs before him; he was crying terribly; and I supposed the lambs were skittish and would not be guided.

"'What is the matter, my little man?' I asked.

"'There's Heathcliff and a woman, yonder, under t' Nab,' he blubbered, 'un' I darnut pass 'em.'"

It is there, the end, in one line, charged with the vibration of the supernatural. One line that carries the suggestion of I know not what ghostly and immaterial passion and its unearthly satisfaction.

* * * * *

And this book stands alone, absolutely self-begotten and self-born. It belongs to no school; it follows no tendency. You cannot put it into any category. It is not "Realism", it is not "Romance", any more than *Jane Eyre*: and if any other master's method, De Maupassant's or Turgeniev's, is to be the test, it will not stand it. There is nothing in it you can seize and name. You will not find in it support for any creed or theory. The redemption of Catherine Linton and Hareton is thrown in by the way in sheer opulence of imagination. It is not insisted on. Redemption is not the keynote of *Wuthering Heights*. The moral problem never entered into Emily Brontë's head. You may call her what you will—Pagan, pantheist, transcendentalist mystic and worshipper of earth, she slips from all your formulas. She reveals a point of view above good and evil. Hers is an attitude of tolerance that is only not tenderness because her acceptance of life and of all that lives is unqualified and unstinting. It is too lucid and too high for pity.

Heathcliff and Catherine exist. They justify their existence by their passion. But if you ask what is to be said for such a creature as Linton Heathcliff, you will be told that he does not justify his existence; his existence justifies him.

> Do I despise the timid deer,
> Because his limbs are fleet with fear?
> Or, would I mock the wolf's death-howl,
> Because his form is gaunt and foul?
> Or, hear with joy the lev'ret's cry,
> Because it cannot bravely die?
> No! Then above his memory
> Let Pity's heart as tender be.

After all it *is* pity; it is tenderness.

And if Emily Brontë stands alone and is at her greatest in the things that none but she can do, she is great also in some that she may be said to share with other novelists; the drawing of minor characters, for instance. Lockwood may be a little indistinct, but he is properly so, for he is not a character, he is a mere impersonal looker-on. But Nelly Dean, the chief teller of the story, preserves her rich individuality through all the tortuous windings of the tale. Joseph, the old farm-servant, the bitter, ranting Calvinist, is a masterpiece. And masterly was that inspiration that made Joseph chorus to a drama that moves above good and evil. "'Thank Hivin for all!'" says Joseph. "All warks togither for gooid, to them as is chozzen and piked out fro' the rubbidge. Yah knaw whet t' Scripture sez.'" "'It's a blazing shame, that I cannot oppen t' blessed Book, but yah set up them glories to Sattan, and all t' flaysome wickednesses that iver were born into the warld.'"

Charlotte Brontë said of her sister: "Though her feeling for the people round her was benevolent, intercourse with them she never sought; nor, with very few exceptions, ever experienced

… she could hear of them with interest and talk of them with detail, minute, graphic, and accurate; but *with* them she rarely exchanged a word." And yet you might have said she had been listening to Joseph all her life, such is her command of his copious utterance: "'Ech! ech!' exclaimed Joseph. 'Weel done, Miss Cathy! weel done, Miss Cathy! Howsiver, t' maister sall just tum'le o'er them brocken pots; un' then we's hear summut; we's hear how it's to be. Gooid-for-naught madling! ye desarve pining fro' this to Churstmas, flinging t' precious gifts o' God under fooit i' yer flaysome rages! But I'm mista'en if ye shew yer sperrit lang. Will Hathecliff bide sich bonny ways, think ye? I nobbut wish he may catch ye i' that plisky. I nobbut wish he may.'"

Edgar Linton is weak in drawing and in colour; but it was well-nigh impossible to make him more alive beside Catherine and Heathcliff. If Emily's hand fails in Edgar Linton it gains strength again in Isabella. These two are the types of the civilized, the over-refined, the delicate wearers of silk and velvet, dwellers in drawing-rooms with pure white ceilings bordered with gold, "with showers of glass-drops hanging in silver chains from the centre". They, as surely as the tainted Hindley, are bound to perish in any struggle with strong, fierce, primeval flesh and blood. The fatal moment in the tale is where the two half-savage children, Catherine and Heathcliff, come to Thrushcross Grange. Thrushcross Grange, with all its sickly brood, is doomed to go down before Wuthering Heights. But Thrushcross Grange is fatal to Catherine too. She has gone far from reality when she is dazzled by the glittering glass-drops and the illusion of Thrushcross Grange. She has divorced her body from her soul for a little finer living, for a polished, a scrupulously clean, perfectly presentable husband.

Emily Brontë shows an unerring psychology in her handling of the relations between Isabella and Catherine. It is Isabella's morbid passion for Heathcliff that wakes the devil in Catherine. Isabella is a sentimentalist, and she is convinced that Heathcliff would love her if Catherine would "let him". She refuses to believe that Heathcliff is what he is. But Catherine, who *is* Heathcliff, can afford to accuse him. "'Nelly,'" she says, "'help me to convince her of her madness. Tell her what Heathcliff is.... He's not a rough diamond—a pearl-containing oyster of a rustic; he's a fierce, pitiless, wolfish man.'" But Isabella will not believe it. "'Mr. Heathcliff is not a fiend,'" she says; "'he has an honourable soul, and a true one, or how could he remember her?'" It is the same insight that made George Meredith represent Juliana, the sentimental passionist, as declaring her belief in Evan Harrington's innocence while Rose Jocelyn, whose love is more spiritual and therefore more profoundly loyal, doubts. Emily Brontë, like George Meredith, saw a sensualist in every sentimentalist; and Isabella Linton was a little animal under her silken skin. She is ready to go to her end *quand même*, whatever Heathcliff is, but she tricks herself into believing that he is what he is not, that her sensualism may justify itself to her refinement. That is partly why Heathcliff, who is no sensualist, hates and loathes Isabella and her body.

But there are moments when he also hates the body of Catherine that betrayed her. Emily Brontë is unswerving in her drawing of Heathcliff. It is of a piece with his strangeness, his unexpectedness, that he does not hate Edgar Linton with anything like the same intensity of hatred that he has for Isabella. And it is of a piece with his absolute fiery cleanness that never for a moment does he think of taking the lover's obvious revenge. For it is not, I imagine, that Emily Brontë deliberately shirked the issue, or deliberately rejected it; it is that that issue never entered her head. Nor do I see here, in his abandonment of the obvious, any proof of the childlikeness and innocence of Emily, however childlike and innocent she may have been. I see only a tremendous artistic uprightness, the rejection, conscious or unconscious, of an unfitting because extraneous element. Anne, who was ten times more childlike and innocent than Emily, tackles this peculiar obviousness unashamed, because she needed it. And because she did not need it, Emily let it go.

The evil wrought by Heathcliff, like the passion that inspired and tortured him, is an unearthly thing. Charlotte showed insight when she said in her preface to *Wuthering Heights*: "Heathcliff betrays one solitary human feeling, and that is *not* his love for Catherine; which is a sentiment fierce and inhuman ... the single link that connects Heathcliff with humanity is his rudely confessed regard for Hareton Earnshaw—the young man whom he has ruined; and then his half-implied esteem for Nelly Dean." But that Heathcliff is wholly inhuman—"a ghoul, an afreet"—I cannot really see. Emily's psychology here is perforce half on the unearthly plane; it is above our criticism, lending itself to no ordinary tests. But for all his unearthliness, Heathcliff is poignantly human, from his childhood when he implored Nelly Dean to make him "decent", for he is "going to be good", to his last hour of piteous dependence on her. You are not allowed for a moment to forget, that, horrible and vindictive as he is, the child Heathcliff is yet a child. Take the scene where the boy first conceives his vengeance.

"On my inquiring the subject of his thoughts, he answered gravely:

"'I'm trying to settle how I shall pay Hindley back. I don't care how long I wait, if I can only do it at last. I hope he will not die before I do!'

"'For shame, Heathcliff!' said I. 'It is for God to punish wicked people. We should learn to forgive.'

"'No, God won't have the satisfaction that I shall,' he returned. 'I only wish I knew the best way! Let me alone, and I'll plan it out: while I'm thinking of that I don't feel pain.'"

It is very like Heathcliff. It is also pathetically like a child.

In Hareton Earnshaw Emily Brontë is fairly on the earth all the time, and nothing could be finer than her handling of this half-brutalized, and wholly undeveloped thing, her showing of the slow dawn of his feelings and intelligence. Her psychology is never psychologic. The creature reveals himself at each moment of his unfolding for what he is. It was difficult; for in his degradation he had a certain likeness in unlikeness to the degraded Heathcliff. It was Heathcliff's indomitable will that raised him. Hareton cannot rise without a woman's hand to help him. The younger Catherine again was difficult, because of her likeness to her mother. Her temper, her vanity, her headstrong trickiness are Catherine Earnshaw. But Catherine Linton is a healthy animal, incapable of superhuman passion, capable only (when properly chastened by adversity) of quite ordinary pity and devotion. She inspires bewilderment, but terror and fascination never; and never the glamour, the magic evoked by the very name of Catherine Earnshaw. Her escapades and fantasies, recalling Catherine Earnshaw, are all on an attenuated scale.

Yet Catherine Earnshaw seems now and then a less solid figure. That is because her strength does not lie in solidity at all. She is a thing of flame and rushing wind. One half of her is akin to the storms of Wuthering Heights, the other belongs to her unseen abiding-place. Both sides of her are immortal.

And they are of that immortality which is the spirit of place—the spirit that, more than all spirits, inspired Emily Brontë. Two of Charlotte's books, *The Professor* and *Villette*, might have been written away from Haworth; Emily's owes much of its outward character to the moors, where it was brought forth. Not even Charlotte could paint, could suggest scenes like Emily Brontë. There is nobody to compare with her but Thomas Hardy; and even he has to labour more, to put in more strokes to achieve his effect. In four lines she gives the storm, the cold and savage foreground, and the distance of the Heights: "One may guess the power of the north wind blowing over the edge, by the excessive slant of a few stunted firs at the end of the house; and by a range of gaunt thorns, all stretching their limbs one way, as if craving alms of the sun."

See the finish of this landscape, framed in a window: "They sat together in a window whose lattice lay back against the wall, and displayed, beyond the garden trees and the wild green park, the valley of Gimmerton, with a long line of mist winding nearly to its top (for very soon after you pass the chapel, as you may have noticed, the sough that runs from the marshes joins a beck which follows the bend of the glen). Wuthering Heights rose above this silvery vapour; but our old house was invisible; it rather dips down on the other side."

In six lines she can paint sound, and distance, and scenery, and the turn of the seasons, and the two magics of two atmospheres. "Gimmerton chapel bells were still ringing; and the full, mellow flow of the beck in the valley came soothingly on the ear. It was a sweet substitute for the yet absent murmur of the summer foliage, which drowned that music about the Grange when the trees were in leaf. At Wuthering Heights it always sounded on quiet days following a great thaw or a season of steady rain."

That music is the prelude to Heathcliff's return, and to the passionate scene that ends in Catherine's death.

And nothing could be more vivid, more concrete, than Emily Brontë's method. Time is marked as a shepherd on the moors might mark it, by the movement of the sun, the moon, and the stars; by weather, and the passage of the seasons. Passions, emotions, are always presented in bodily symbols, by means of the bodily acts and violences they inspire. The passing of the invisible is made known in the same manner. And the visible world moves and shines and darkens with an absolute illusion of reality. Here is a road seen between sunset and moonrise: "... all that remained of day was a beamless amber light along the west: but I could see every pebble on the path, and every blade of grass, by the light of that splendid moon".

The book has faults, many and glaring faults. You have to read it many times before you can realize in the mass its amazing qualities. For it is probably the worst-constructed tale that ever was written, this story of two houses and of three generations that the man Lockwood is supposed to tell. Not only has Lockwood to tell of things he could not possibly have heard and seen, but sometimes you get scene within vivid scene, dialogue within dialogue, and tale within tale, four deep. Sometimes you are carried back in a time and sometimes forward. You have to think hard before you know for certain whose wife Catherine Heathcliff really is. You cannot get over Lockwood's original mistake. And this poor device of narrative at second-hand, third-hand, fourth-hand, is used to convey things incredible, inconceivable; all the secret, invisible drama of the souls of Catherine and Heathcliff, as well as whole acts of the most visible, the most tangible, the most direct and vivid and tumultuous drama; drama so tumultuous, so vivid, and so direct, that by no possibility could it have been conveyed by any medium. It simply happens.

And that is how Emily Brontë's genius triumphs over all her faults. It is not only that you forgive her faults and forget them, you are not—in the third reading anyhow—aware of them. They disappear, they are destroyed, they are burnt up in her flame, and you wonder how you ever saw them. All her clumsy contrivances cannot stay her course, or obscure her light, or quench her fire. Things happen before your eyes, and it does not matter whether Lockwood, or Nelly Dean, or Heathcliff, or Catherine, tells you of their happening.

And yet, though Lockwood and Nelly Dean are the thinnest, the most transparent of pure mediums, they preserve their personalities throughout. Nelly especially. The tale only begins to move when Lockwood drops out and Nelly takes it up. At that point Emily Brontë's style becomes assured in its directness and simplicity, and thenceforward it never falters or changes its essential character.

And it is there, first of all, in that unfaltering, unchanging quality of style that she stands so far above her sister. She has no purple patches, no decorative effects. No dubiously shining rhetoric is hers. She does not deal in metaphors or in those ponderous abstractions, those dreadful second-hand symbolic figures—Hope, Imagination, Memory, and the rest of them, that move with every appearance of solidity in Charlotte's pages. There are no angels in her rainbows. Her "grand style" goes unclothed, perfect in its naked strength, its naked beauty. It is not possible to praise Charlotte's style without reservations; it is not always possible to give passages that illustrate her qualities without suppressing her defects. What was a pernicious habit with Charlotte, her use of words like "peruse", "indite", "retain", with Emily is a mere slip of the pen. There are only, I think, three of such slips in *Wuthering Heights*. Charlotte was capable of mixing her worst things with her best. She mixed them most in her dialogue, where sins of style are sinfullest. It is not always possible to give a scene, word for word, from Charlotte's novels; the dramatic illusion, the illusion of reality, is best preserved by formidable cutting.

But not only was Emily's style sinless; it is on the whole purest, most natural, and most inevitable in her dialogue; and that, although the passions she conceived were so tremendous, so unearthly, that she might have been pardoned if she found no human speech to render them.

What is more, her dramatic instinct never fails her as it fails Charlotte over and over again. Charlotte had not always the mastery and self-mastery that, having worked a situation up to its dramatic climax, leaves it there. A certain obscure feeling for rightness guides her in the large, striding movement of the drama; it is in the handling of the scenes that she collapses. She wanders from climax to climax; she goes back on her own trail; she ruins her best effects by repetition. She has no continuous dramatic instinct; no sense whatever of dramatic form.

These are present somehow in *Wuthering Heights*, in spite of its monstrous formlessness. Emily may have had no more sense of form for form's sake than Charlotte; she may have had no more dramatic instinct; but she had an instinct for the ways of human passion. She knew that passion runs its course, from its excitement to its climax and exhaustion. It has a natural beginning and a natural end. And so her scenes of passion follow nature. She never goes back on her effect, never urges passion past its climax, or stirs it in its exhaustion. In this she is a greater "realist" than Charlotte.

* * * * *

It is incredible that *Wuthering Heights*, or any line of it, any line that Emily Brontë ever wrote, should have passed for Charlotte's. She did things that Charlotte could never have done if she tried a thousand years, things not only incomparably greater, but unique.

Yet in her lifetime she was unrecognized. What is true of her prose is true also of her poems. They, indeed, did bring her a little praise, obscure and momentary. No less she was unrecognized to such an extent that *Wuthering Heights* was said and believed to be an immature work of Charlotte's. Even after her death, her eulogist, Sydney Dobell, was so far from recognizing her, that he seems to have had a lingering doubt as to Ellis Bell's identity until Charlotte convinced him of his error.

And only the other day a bold attempt was made to tear from Emily Brontë the glory that she has won at last from time. The very latest theory,[A] offered to the world as a marvellous discovery, the fruit of passionate enthusiasm and research, is the old, old theory that Charlotte, and not Emily, wrote *Wuthering Heights*. And Sydney Dobell, with his little error, is made to serve as a witness. In order to make out a case for Charlotte, the enthusiast and researcher is obliged to disparage every other work of Emily's. He leans rashly enough on the assumption that her "Gondal Chronicles" were, in their puerility, beneath contempt, still more rashly on his own opinion that she was no poet.

[Footnote A: *The Key to the Brontë Works*, by J. Malham-Dembleby. See Appendix I.]

If this were the only line he took, this amusing theorist might be left alone. The publication of the *Complete Poems* settles him. The value, the really priceless value, of his undertaking is in the long array of parallel passages from the prose of Charlotte and of Emily with which he endeavours to support it. For, so far from supporting it, these columns are the most convincing, the most direct and palpable refutation of his theory. If any uncritical reader should desire to see for himself wherein Charlotte and Emily Brontë differed; in what manner, with what incompatible qualities and to what an immeasurable degree the younger sister was pre-eminent, he cannot do better than study those parallel passages. If ever there was a voice, a quality, an air absolutely apart and distinct, not to be approached by, or confounded with any other, it is Emily Brontë's.

It was the glare of Charlotte's fame that caused in her lifetime that blindness and confusion. And Emily, between pride and a superb indifference, suffered it. She withdrew, with what seemed an obstinate perversity, into her own magnificent obscurity. She never raised a hand to help herself. She left no record, not a note or a word to prove her authorship of *Wuthering Heights*. Until the appearance in 1910 of her *Complete Poems* the world had no proof of it but Charlotte's statement. It was considered enough, in Charlotte's lifetime. The world accepted her disclaimer.

But the trouble began again after Charlotte's death. Emily herself had no legend; but her genius was perpetually the prey of rumours that left her personality untouched. Among the many provoked by Mrs. Gaskell's *Life*, there was one attributing *Wuthering Heights* to her brother Branwell. [A] Mr. Francis Grundy said that Branwell told him he had written *Wuthering Heights*. Mr. Leyland believed Mr. Grundy. He believed that Branwell was a great poet and a great novelist, and he wrote two solid volumes of his own in support of his belief.

[Footnote A: The curious will find a note on this point in Appendix II.]

Nobody believes in Mr. Grundy, or in Mr. Leyland and his

belief in Branwell now. All that can be said of Branwell, in understanding and extenuation, is that he would have been a great poet and a greater novelist if he could have had his own way.

This having of your own way, unconsciously, undeliberately, would seem to be the supreme test of genius. Having your own way in the teeth of circumstances, of fathers and of brothers, and of aunts, of school-mistresses,[A] and of French professors, of the parish, of poverty, of public opinion and hereditary disease; in the teeth of the most disastrous of all hindrances, duty, not neglected, but fulfilled. By this test the genius of Emily Brontë fairly flames; Charlotte's stands beside it with a face hidden at times behind bruised and darkened wings. By this test even Anne's pale talent shows here and there a flicker as of fire. In all three the having of their own way was, after all, the great submission, the ultimate obedience to destiny.

[Footnote A: It was Miss Wooler who taught Charlotte to "peruse".]

For genius like theirs *is* destiny. And that brings us back to the eternal question of the Sources. "Experience" will not account for what was greatest in Charlotte. It will hardly account for what was least in Emily. With her only the secret, the innermost experience counted. If the sources of *Wuthering Heights* are in the "Gondal Poems", the sources of the poems are in *that* experience, in the long life of her adventurous spirit. Her genius, like Henry Angora and Rosina and the rest of them, flew from the "Palaces of Instruction". As she *was* Henry Angora, so she *was* Heathcliff and Catherine Earnshaw.

It is a case of "The Horse I rode at the battle of Zamorna", that is all.

There has been too much talk about experience. What the critic, the impressionist, of the Brontës needs is to recover, before all things, the innocence of the eye. No doubt we all of us had it once, and can remember more or less what it was like. To those who have lost it I would say: Go back and read again Mrs. Gaskell's *Life of Charlotte Brontë*.

Years and years ago, when I was a child, hunting forlornly in my father's bookshelves, I came upon a small, shabby volume, bound in yellow linen. The title-page was adorned with one bad wood-cut that showed a grim, plain house standing obliquely to a churchyard packed with tombstones—tombstones upright and flat, and slanting at all angles. In the foreground was a haycock, where the grave grass had been mown. I do not know how the artist, whose resources were of the slenderest, contrived to get his overwhelming but fascinating effect of moorland solitude, of black-grey nakedness and abiding gloom. But he certainly got it and gave it. There was one other picture, representing a memorial tablet.

Tombstones always fascinated me in those days, because I was mortally afraid of them; and I opened that book and read it through.

I could not, in fact, put it down. For the first time I was in the grip of a reality more poignant than any that I had yet known, of a tragedy that I could hardly bear. I suppose I have read that book a score of times since then. There are pages in it that I shrink from approaching even now, because of the agony of realization they revive. The passing bell tolled continually in the prelude; it sounded at intervals throughout; it tolled again at the close. The refrain of "Here lie the Remains" haunted me like a dolorous song. It seemed to me a decorous and stately accompaniment to such a tale, and that wood-cut on the title-page a fitting ornament. I knew every corner of that house. I have an impression (it is probably a wrong one) of a flagged path going right down from the Parsonage door through another door and plunging among the tombs. I saw six little white and wistful faces looking out of an upper window; I saw six little children going up and up a lane, and I wondered how the tiny feet of babies ever got so far. I saw six little Brontë babies lost in the spaces of the illimitable moors. They went over rough stones and walls and mountain torrents; their absurd petticoats were blown upwards by the wind, and their feet were tangled in the heather. They struggled and struggled, and yet were in an ecstasy that I could well understand.

I remember I lingered somewhat long over the schooldays at Cowan Bridge and that I found the Brussels period dull; M. Héger struck me as a tiresome pedant, and I wondered how Charlotte could ever have put up with him. There was a great deal about Branwell that I could not understand at all, and so forgot. And I skipped all the London part, and Charlotte's literary letters. I had a very vague idea of Charlotte apart from Haworth and the moors, from the Parsonage and the tombstones, from Tabby and Martha and the little black cat that died, from the garden where she picked the currants, and the quiet rooms where she wrote her wonderful, wonderful books.

But, for all that skipping and forgetting, there stood out a vivid and ineffaceable idea of Emily; Emily who was tall and strong and unconquerable; Emily who loved animals, and loved the moors; Emily and Keeper, that marvellous dog; Emily kneading bread with her book propped before her; Emily who was Ellis Bell, listening contemptuously to the reviews of *Wuthering Heights*; Emily stitching at the long seam with dying fingers; and Emily dead, carried down the long, flagged path, with Keeper following in the mourners' train.

And, all through, an invisible, intangible presence, something mysterious, but omnipotently alive; something that excited these three sisters; something that atoned, that not only consoled for suffering and solitude and bereavement, but that drew its strength from these things; something that moved in this book like the soul of it; something that they called "genius".

Now that, as truly as I can set it down, is the impression conveyed to a child's mind by Mrs. Gaskell's *Life of Charlotte Brontë*. And making some deductions for a child's morbid attraction to tombstones, and a child's natural interest in children, it seems to me even now that this innocent impression is the true one. It eliminates the inessential and preserves the proportions; above all, it preserves the figure of Emily Brontë, solitary and unique.

Anyhow, I have never been able to get away from it.

September 1911.

APPENDIX I

THE KEY TO THE BRONTË WORKS

More than once Mr. Malham-Dembleby has approached us with his mysterious "Key". There was his "Key to *Jane Eyre*", published in the *Saturday Review* in 1902; there was his "Lifting of the Brontë Veil", published in the *Fortnightly Review* in 1907; and there was the correspondence that followed. Now he has gathered all his evidence together into one formidable book, and we are faced with what he calls his "miraculous and sensational" discovery that it was Charlotte and not Emily Brontë who wrote *Wuthering Heights*, and that in *Wuthering Heights* she immortalized the great tragic passion of her life, inspired by M. Héger, who, if you please, is Heathcliff.

This is Mr. Malham-Dembleby's most important contribution to the subject. M. Héger, Mr. Malham-Dembleby declares, was Heathcliff before he was M. Pelet, or Rochester, or M. Paul. And as it was Charlotte and not Emily who experienced passion, Charlotte alone was able to immortalize it.

So much Mr. Malham-Dembleby assumes in the interests of psychology. But it is not from crude psychological arguments that he forges his tremendous Key. It is from the internal evidence of the works, supported by much "sensational" matter from the outside.

By way of internal evidence then, we have first the sensational discovery of a work, *Gleanings in Craven, or The Tourists' Guide*, by "one Frederic Montagu", published at Skipton-in-Craven in

1838, which work the author of *Wuthering Heights* and *Jane Eyre* must have read and drawn upon for many things, names (including her own pseudonym of Currer Bell), descriptions of scenery, local legends, as of that fairy Jannet, Queen of the Malhamdale Elves, who haunted the sources of the Aire and suggested Rochester's Queen of Elves, his fairy, Janet Eyre. Parallel passages are given showing a certain correspondence between Montagu's traveller's tale and the opening scene of *Wuthering Heights*. Montagu goes on horseback to a solitary house, like Lockwood, and, like Lockwood, is shown to bed, dreams, and is awakened by a white-faced apparition (his hostess, not his host), who holds a lighted candle, like Heathcliff, and whose features, like Heathcliff's, are convulsed with diabolical rage, and so on. Mr. Malham-Dembleby, in a third parallel column, uses the same phrases to describe Jane Eyre's arrival at Rochester's house, her dreams, and the appearance of Rochester's mad wife at her bedside; his contention being that the two scenes are written by the same hand.

All this is very curious and interesting; so far, however, Mr. Malham-Dembleby's sensational evidence does no more for us than suggest that Charlotte and Emily may very likely have read Montagu's book.

But the plot thickens. Mr. Malham-Dembleby first prints parallel passages from Montagu's book and *Wuthering Heights* and *Jane Eyre*, then, extensively, scene after scene from *Jane Eyre* and *Wuthering Heights*.

Some of these coincidences seem on the first blush of it remarkable, for instance, the child-phantom which appears both to Jane Eyre and to Nelly Dean in *Wuthering Heights*; or the rainy day and the fireside scene, which occur in the third chapter of *Wuthering Heights* and the opening chapter of *Jane Eyre*. Others again, such as the parallel between the return of Heathcliff to Catherine and that of Jane to Rochester, will not bear examination for a moment. Of this and most of Mr. Malham-Dembleby's parallels it may be said that they only maintain their startling character by the process of tearing words from their sentences, sentences from their contexts, contexts from their scenes, and scenes from the living body of each book. Apparently to Mr. Malham-Dembleby, a book, at any rate a Brontë book, is not a living body; each is a box of German bricks, and he takes all the boxes and tumbles them out on the floor together and rearranges them so as to show that, after all, there was only one box of bricks in the family, and that was Charlotte's. Much of his argument and the force of his parallel passages depends on the identification of the characters in the Brontë works, not only with their assumed originals, but with each other. For Mr. Malham-Dembleby's purposes poor M. Héger, a model already remorselessly overworked by Charlotte, has to sit, not only for M. Pelet, for Rochester and Yorke Hunsden, for Robert and for Louis Moore, but for Heathcliff, and, if you would believe it, for Hareton Earnshaw; because (parallel passage!) the younger Catherine and Hareton Earnshaw were teacher and pupil, and so (when she taught him English) were Charlotte and M. Héger.

Mr. Malham-Dembleby's work of identification is made easier for him by his subsidiary discovery of Charlotte's two methods, Method I, interchange of the sex; Method II, alteration of the age of her characters. With this licence almost any character may be any other. Thus Hareton Earnshaw looking at Catherine is Jane Eyre looking at Mr. Rochester. When he touches her Nelly Dean says, "He might have stuck a knife into her, she started in such a taking"; and Rochester says to Jane, "You stick a sly penknife under my ear" (parallel passage!). Lockwood at Wuthering Heights is Jane Eyre at Thornton Hall; Heathcliff appearing at Lockwood's bedside, besides being M. Héger and Rochester, is Rochester's mad wife. Heathcliff returning to Catherine is Jane returning to Rochester, and so on. But however varied, however apparently discriminated the characters, M. Héger is in all the men, and Charlotte is in all the women, in the two Catherines, in Jane Eyre and Frances Henri; in Caroline Helstone, in Pauline Bassompierre, and Lucy Snowe.

Now there is a certain plausibility in this. With all their vividness and individuality Charlotte Brontë's characters have a way of shading off into each other. Jane has much in common with Frances and with Lucy, and Lucy with Pauline. Her men incline rather to one type, that of the masterful, arbitrary, instructive male; that is the type she likes best to draw. Yorke Hunsden in *The Professor* splits up into Rochester and Robert Moore and Mr. Yorke; and there is a certain amount of Paul Emanuel in all of them. But life gives us our types very much that way, and there is a bit of somebody else in everybody. It is easy to suggest identity by exaggerating small points of resemblance and suppressing large and essential differences (which is what Mr. Malham-Dembleby does all the time). But take each whole living man and woman as they have been created for us, I don't care if Catherine Earnshaw and Jane Eyre *did* each have a fit of passion in a locked room, and if a servant waited upon each with gruel; there is no earthly likeness between the soul of Catherine and the soul of Jane. I don't care if there was "hell-light" in Rochester's eyes and Heathcliff's too, if they both swore by the "Deuce", and had both swarthy complexions like Paul Emanuel; for there is a whole universe between Heathcliff and Rochester, between Rochester and M. Paul. Beside Heathcliff, that Titan raging on a mountain-top, M. Paul is merely a little man gesticulating on an *estrade*.

So much for the identifications. Mr. Malham-Dembleby has been tempted to force them thus, because they support his theory of M. Héger and of the great tragic passion, as his theory, by a vicious circle, supports his identifications. His procedure is to quote all the emotional passages he can lay his hands on, from the *Poems*, from *Wuthering Heights*, from *Jane Eyre*, from *Villette* and *The Professor*, "... all her life's hope was torn by the roots out of her own riven and outraged heart..." (*Villette*) "... faith was blighted, confidence destroyed..." (*Jane Eyre*) ... "Mr. Rochester" (M. Héger, we are informed in confidential brackets) was not "what she had thought him". Assuring us that Charlotte was here describing her own emotions, he builds his argument. "Evidence" (the evidence of these passages) "shows it was in her dark season when Charlotte Brontë wrote *Wuthering Heights*, and that she portrayed M. Héger therein with all the vindictiveness of a woman with 'a riven, outraged heart', the wounds in which yet rankled sorely." So that, key in hand, for "that ghoul Heathcliff!" we must read "that ghoul Héger". We must believe that *Wuthering Heights* was written in pure vindictiveness, and that Charlotte Brontë repudiated its authorship for three reasons: because it contained "too humiliating a story" of her "heart-thrall"; because of her subsequent remorse (proof, the modified animus of her portrait of M. Héger as Rochester and as M. Paul), and for certain sound business considerations. So much for internal evidence.

Not that Mr. Malham-Dembleby relies on it altogether. He draws largely upon legend and conjecture, and on more "sensational discoveries" of his own. He certainly succeeds in proving that legend and conjecture in Brussels began at a very early date. Naturally enough it fairly flared after the publication of *Jane Eyre*. So far there is nothing new in his discoveries. But he does provide a thrill when he unearths Eugène Sue's extinct novel of *Miss Mary, ou l'Institutrice*, and gives us parallel passages from that. For in *Miss Mary*, published in 1850-51[A] we have, not only character for character and scene for scene, "lifted" bodily from *Jane Eyre*, but the situation in *The Professor* and *Villette* is largely anticipated. We are told that Eugène Sue was in Brussels in 1844, the year in which Charlotte left the Pensionnat. This is interesting. But what does it prove? Not, I think, what Mr. Malham-Dembleby maintains—that M. Héger made indiscreet revelations to Eugène Sue, but that Eugène Sue was an unscrupulous plagiarist who took his own where he found it, either in the pages of *Jane Eyre* or in the tittle-tattle of a Brussels salon. However indiscreet M. Héger may have been, he was a man of proved gravity and honour. He would, at any rate, have drawn the line at frivolous treachery. Nobody, however, can answer for what Madame Héger and her friends may not have said. Which disposes of Eugène Sue.

[Footnote A: Serially in the *London Journal* in 1850; in volume form in Paris, 1851. It is possible, but not likely, that Eugène Sue may have seen the manuscript of *The Professor* when it was "going the round".]

Then there is that other "sensational discovery" of the Héger portrait, that little drawing (now in the National Portrait Gallery) of Charlotte Brontë in curls, wearing a green gown, and reading *Shirley*. It is signed Paul Héger, 1850, the year of *Shirley's* publication, and the year in which Charlotte sat to Richmond for her portrait. There are two inscriptions on the back: "The Wearin' of the Green; First since Emily's death"; and below: "This drawing is by P. Héger, done from life in 1850." The handwriting gives no clue.

Mr. Malham-Dembleby attaches immense importance to this green gown, which he "identifies" with the pink one worn by Lucy in *Villette*. He says that Lady Ritchie told him that Charlotte wore a green gown at the dinner-party Thackeray gave for her in June, 1850; and when the green gown turns out after all to be a white one with a green pattern on it, it is all one to Mr. Malham-Dembleby. So much for the green gown. Still, gown or no gown, the portrait *may* be genuine. Mr. Malham-Dembleby says that it is drawn on the same paper as that used in Mr. George Smith's house, where Charlotte was staying in June 1850, and he argues that Charlotte and M. Héger met in London that year, and that he then drew this portrait of her from the life. True, the portrait is a very creditable performance for an amateur; true, M. Héger's children maintained that their father did not draw, and there is no earthly evidence that he did; true, we have nothing but one person's report of another person's (a collector's) statement that he had obtained the portrait from the Héger family, a statement at variance with the evidence of the Héger family itself. But granted that the children of M. Héger were mistaken as to their father's gift, and that he did draw this portrait of Charlotte Brontë from Charlotte herself in London in 1850, I cannot see that it matters a straw or helps us to the assumption of the great tragic passion which is the main support of Mr. Malham-Dembleby's amazing fabrication.

APPENDIX II

Leyland's theory is that Branwell Brontë wrote the first seventeen chapters of *Wuthering Heights*. It has very little beyond Leyland's passionate conviction to support it. There is a passage in a letter of Branwell's to Leyland, the sculptor, written in 1845, where he says he is writing a three-volume novel of which the first volume is completed. He compares it with "Hamlet" and with "Lear". There is also Branwell's alleged statement to Mr. Grundy. And there is an obscure legend of manuscripts produced from Branwell's hat, before the eyes of Mr. Grundy, in an inn-parlour. Leyland argues freely from the antecedent probability suggested by Branwell's letters and his verse, which he published by way of vindication. He could hardly have done Branwell a worse service. Branwell's letters give us a vivid idea of the sort of manuscripts that would be produced, in inn-parlours, from his hat. As for his verse—that formless, fluent gush of sentimentalism—it might have passed as an error of his youth, but for poor Leyland's comments on its majesty and beauty. There are corpses in it and tombstones, and girls dying of tuberculosis, obscured beyond recognition in a mush of verbiage. There is not a live line in it. One sonnet only, out of Branwell's many sonnets, is fitted to survive. It has a certain melancholy, sentimental grace. But it is not a good sonnet, and it shows Branwell at his best. At his worst he sinks far below Charlotte at her worst, and, compared with Emily or with Charlotte at her best, Branwell is nowhere. Even Anne beats him. Her sad, virginal restraint gives a certain form and value to her colourless and slender gift.

There is a psychology of such things, as there is a psychology of works of genius. Emily Brontë's work, with all its faults of construction, shows one and indivisible, fused in one fire from first to last. One cannot take the first seventeen chapters of *Wuthering Heights* and separate them from the rest. There is no faltering anywhere and no break in the power and the passion of this stupendous tale. And where passion is, sentimentalism is not. And there is not anywhere in *Wuthering Heights* a trace of that corruption which for the life of him Branwell could not have kept out of the manuscripts he produced from his hat.

www.ingramcontent.com/pod-product-compliance
Lightning Source LLC
Chambersburg PA
CBHW030108170426
43198CB00009B/543